HOW TO
ASSESS
THE VOCATIONAL
CURRICULUM

D1100397

HOW TO
ASSESS
THE VOCATIONAL
CURRICULUM

KATHRYN ECCLESTONE

**KOGAN
PAGE**

Also published by Kogan Page

Change Through Networking in Vocational Education, Tony Nasta
Vocational Education and the Adult Unwaged, Jenny Hunt and Heather Jackson
The Work-related Curriculum, edited by Jerry Wellington
How to Design a Vocational Curriculum, Tony Nasta

First published in 1996

Kogan Page Limited
120 Pentonville Road
London N1 9JN

British Library Cataloguing in Publication Data

A CIP record for this book is available from the British Library.

ISBN 0 7494 1706 4

Typeset by Kogan Page
Printed and bound in Great Britain by Biddles Ltd, Guildford and King's Lynn

Contents

Acknowledgements

I am grateful for the feedback skills of colleagues and students who have spent time discussing some of the issues raised during the research and writing of this book. In particular, I would like to thank Tony Nasta and Les August for their insights about assessment in colleges; Toni Fazeli for ideas about assessing adult learners and the effects of bias in assessment; Sue Harrison from South East Derbyshire College for her practical knowledge about assessment in learning and records of achievement; and Larry Hunter from the University of Sunderland for his insights about assessment in school contexts. I would also like to thank Paul Patterson from Northumberland College and Frank Perry from South Tyneside College and the many school, college and university teachers who have shared their knowledge and practice in assessment with me.

Series Editor's Preface

The vocational curriculum is currently under scrutiny and is of close interest to government, employers and educationalists. All have drawn attention to the vital importance of increasing participation rates in post-compulsory education in the UK. The learning needs of neither full-time students, staying on beyond the age of 16, nor the growing number of adult students, are likely to be satisfied through the GCSE and GCE A level routes alone.

Kathryn Ecclestone's book is a valuable addition to this series of texts on the changing vocational curriculum. It is designed for two audiences: teaching staff in schools and colleges seeking advice on how to organize and manage vocational programmes, and student teachers looking for a guide to current developments in vocational education.

The question of how to assess the vocational curriculum has come to prominence with the rapid spread of GNVQs and NVQs as alternatives to GCE A levels and GCSEs. Scarcely a week passes without a pronouncement on assessment from the National Council for Vocational Qualifications (NCVQ), the government, or the examining bodies. *How to Assess the Vocational Curriculum* is a comprehensive guide to this complex area. The growing body of jargon used to describe the assessment process is explained simply so that the reader can quickly get to grips with terms like 'internal verification' and 'the accreditation of prior learning'. The author has a central concern with the needs of students and teachers and the discussion of assessment methods is closely related to the promotion of learning.

Each chapter has been written to stand on its own; the reader who is primarily interested in the assessment of modular courses or credit accumulation and transfer can turn immediately to the relevant page. The chapters follow a broadly similar approach, which includes an explanation of the context of the issue, an evaluation of the practical implications for assessing students and some illustrative examples, where appropriate. The book examines the origins of outcome-based approaches in NVQs and GNVQs and there is a critical discussion of their use and effectiveness.

Tony Nasta, 1996

1 Introduction and Background

Why assessment is becoming more important

Over the past 15 years, assessment has come to play a central role in teaching and learning and in formally recognizing learners' achievements. Changes to the way assessment is used have had profound effects on the way that the vocational curriculum is organized and on teaching and learning methods in schools, colleges and universities. National Vocational Qualifications (NVQs), introduced in 1986, and General National Vocational Qualifications (GNVQs), introduced in 1992, have fundamentally altered our thinking about what assessment should be used for, how we should carry it out and who should benefit from it. This change is particularly evident in the vocational curriculum offered by schools, further education and sixth form colleges and universities, but it is also apparent in other parts of the further and higher education curriculum and in the school National Curriculum.

This more prominent role for assessment can be partly traced to political factors that require institutions to manage assessment more strategically than previously. A series of recent political initiatives and requirements from external bodies have affected how assessment is organized in vocational qualifications. These include:

- Government's National Targets for Education and Training (NTETs), which aim to increase the levels of participation in learning programmes and set specific targets for the achievement of academic and vocational qualifications amongst young people and adults.
- A quality assurance and funding framework for programmes funded by the Further Education Funding Council (FEFC), which places an emphasis on learners' entitlement to different types of assessment at different stages of progression through a learning programme, and relates funding to learners' achievements.
- The growth in opportunities for learners to gain credit for individual units or modules in more flexible combinations, to accumulate these over time and to transfer them between different education and training organizations.

- Requirements for standardized processes for quality assurance in the assessment and accreditation of GNVQs and NVQs.
- The Department for Education and Employment's (DfEE) Student Charter, which has led to colleges and universities setting 'standards' and 'indicators' for learners' entitlement to assessment.
- The statutory requirement for schools and colleges to publish information about learners' achievements and career routes, Published Information on Students' Achievements (PISA).

There have been a number of reviews of assessment in GNVQs commissioned by the Employment Department, the National Council for Vocational Qualifications (NCVQ), the DfEE, the FEFC Inspectorate and the Further Education Development Agency.

Political imperatives are not the only reason for taking assessment more seriously. When it is used well, assement can play a powerful and positive role in motivating learners and in encouraging them to take more control of their learning. Interest in assessment as an integral part of the learning process has fuelled widespread interest among teachers, educational researchers and curriculum development bodies in the educational benefits of assessment. There have been attempts to untangle some of the confusion surrounding assessment, and to clarify the different purposes of assessment. In particular, there is growing interest in using assessment to diagnose learners' needs and provide effective feedback about learning which helps them become independent learners.

Five implications emerge from this political and educational interest:

- Assessment is seen to offer greater potential for motivating learners to be more effective in their learning.
- Decisions about funding and judgements about institutions' performance are increasingly based on the outcomes of assessment.
- Assessment is becoming more technically complex for managers and teachers to administer and implement.
- Colleges, schools and universities are having to adopt a more strategic approach to how they organize and implement assessment.
- Teachers and lecturers need a high level of professional competence and understanding about assessment.

These themes are closely related. Better uses of assessment in learning programmes have enormous implications for teachers and learners in improving the quality of teaching and learning. Increased external requirements for how assessment is organized and implemented raise issues for managers and teachers of the vocational curriculum about how to deal with these effectively, and how to use assessment in learning processes.

New possibilities

There is currently a widespread belief that new forms of assessment in the vocational curriculum will both increase access and levels of participation in education and training, and raise learners' achievements. As a result, there has been an enormous growth in 'formal' assessment leading to certification. This affects groups of learners who have little experience of formal education in the post-compulsory sector. Assessment increasingly takes place in new contexts such as the workplace, and is based upon achievements gained from life and work experiences as well as through education.

To meet these new possibilities, the techniques and processes used in assessment and certification have changed. They are often based on statements by curriculum designers and awarding bodies of what 'outcomes' are being sought, and publicly available criteria or standards which tell learners, assessors and other interested groups such as employers and other education providers how these outcomes will be measured. More vocational programmes are becoming modular, so that learners can gain credits for successfully achieving outcomes in individual units or modules of learning. These technical changes aim to make assessment procedures clearer, more accessible and more accountable.

Raising levels of participation and widening access to assessment and accreditation are cornerstones of recent reforms to the post-16 system generally, and to the vocational curriculum in particular. A widespread commitment among employers and educational organizations to the National Training and Education Targets (NTETs) makes it crucial for organizations to create better access to formal assessment and accreditation. And in order to motivate learners to take part in learning programmes and become more successful at learning, greater emphasis is being placed on the role of assessment in helping learners become more autonomous and self-directed.

Tensions and dilemmas

The history of assessment shows that political and social tensions, as well as educational ones, have always characterized aspirations for what assessment can do for learners and for society as a whole. Gipps (1995) points out that assessment:

> 'is a powerful tool: it can shape curriculum, teaching and learning; it can affect how [students] come to see themselves both as learners and in a more general sense as competent or not; through labelling and sorting... [certificating and selecting] it affects how [students] are viewed by others; it controls access to further education and high status careers... assessment has become increasingly widespread and significant in our education system and shows no sign of going away or losing its power.'

The more prominent role which assessment now plays in the education and training system means that more groups have a vested interest in its outcomes and in the way it is managed in institutions. Funding bodies, political parties, employers, teachers, managers of institutions, education inspectors, auditors – and learners themselves – all have different interests in, and expectations from, assessment. The annual media and political furore over standards in GCE A-levels and GCSEs shows that assessment carries high political stakes. There are different vested interests too in promoting 'academic' learning over 'vocational' learning, or vice versa, as well as in overcoming the vocational/academic divide.

Gipps argues that the role of assessment in teaching, and in the design of the curriculum, is playing a more influential role in education and training systems around the world. In Britain, it is 'undergoing a paradigm shift from psychometrics to a broader model of educational assessment, from a testing and examination culture to an assessment culture'. As a consequence, public debate about assessment shows that it can be confusing and misunderstood. It is clear too, from recent reports, that assessment in NVQs and GNVQs is causing some concern: teachers and managers in colleges, schools and universities are finding difficulties in managing the amount and variety of assessment which seem to be required. This leads to the recognition that, as well as opening up potential for improving learning and greater achievement, assessment creates dilemmas and tensions for those who design, administer and experience it.

Until the advent of the General Certificate of Secondary Education (GCSE), assessment was largely associated, in most people's minds, with tests of skills and knowledge, and with grading learners' achievements by comparing with those of others learners. The main function of the assessment's was to select people for progression into higher or further education, or into employment. As a result, policy and practice in assessment has been heavily influenced by a long tradition of psychometric testing, based on particular ideas about how intelligence and capability could be measured. More recently, the political and professional emphasis has shifted away from a belief that 'scientific' assessment can measure and predict people's intelligence and ability, towards assessment which can provide more detailed information about what they have achieved.

A shift in our expectations of assessment means that more attention is now being given to the role of assessment in diagnosing people's learning needs, and then formally recognizing and describing their achievements. The scope of achievements which can be assessed and accredited has expanded to include a wide range of personal skills and qualities, as well as knowledge, understanding and practical skills.

Being strategic about assessment

A number of reports by the FEFC Inspectorate, the Further Education Development Agency (FEDA) and the Employment Department show that assessment in NVQs and GNVQs has proved technically complicated and cumbersome to administer, especially in interpreting standards of achievement and in managing a large volume and range of assessments. In spite of a great deal of advice about assessment from awarding bodies, the FEFC Inspectorate, FEDA, and the National Council for Vocational Qualifications (NCVQ), many managers and teachers are uncertain about how to deal with assessment. Assessment is not generally as straightforward to manage as much of the guidance and advice about it seem to suggest.

As well as being the subject of some confusion, assessment has become more controversial. Decisions about funding, judgements about the effectiveness of organizational performance and about funding for future developments are increasingly being made on the basis of the outcomes of assessment. Schools, colleges and universities are more accountable through the students' charter, and the NCVQ and the FEFC requirements, to provide regular, fair and consistent assessment. They are also more accountable than previously for monitoring and assuring consistent standards in assessing their learners' achievements.

By adopting a more strategic approach to providing different services for assessment, institutions can help teachers and learners use assessment more productively and efficiently. Colleges, schools and universities have to:

- provide different assessment services, including pre-admissions guidance and diagnostic assessment, assessment and accreditation of prior learning, tutorial reviews of progress, and efficient processing of certification;
- link different procedures for internal verification and evaluation as part of an overall process of quality assurance;
- train, support and update staff who have different roles in assessment and accreditation;
- ensure that assessment is reliable, valid and fair for all learners;
- ways to measure the 'value added' that the vocational curriculum contributes to learners' achievements.

Professional competence in assessment

Interpreting the various purposes of assessment, implementing different assessment regimes, and at the same time using assessment effectively as an aid to learning, requires teachers with high levels of professional competence, knowledge and insight. Teachers are being asked to develop a range of approaches to assessment for the benefit of their learners, and to use increasingly complex systems for recording evidence of achievement. The demands on them have probably never been greater, or the assessment regimes so onerous.

Teachers have to understand the purposes of assessment in order to use and understand it properly and effectively and to implement it at different stages of the learning programme. They have to use a much wider range of methods and contexts for assessing learners' performance than they have done previously, and incorporate formative and diagnostic assessment into their teaching and tutoring activities. In some programmes they might be required simply to administer external tests in GNVQs, whilst in others, such as a vocational degree programme, they might also be responsible for the design, administration and marking of tests and examinations.

In making judgements about the quality of learners' performance, teachers have to share and moderate their judgements with colleagues, liaise with awarding body verifiers, moderators and external examiners and then present information about learners' achievements to different audiences, such as employers, further and higher education admissions tutors, and funding bodies.

Awarding bodies and managers of institutions therefore have the difficult task of striking a balance between giving teachers extensive guidelines to implement different systems, and fostering their professional understanding and insight into the broader principles which underpin them.

Summary

Assessment plays a pivotal role in the vocational curriculum. New forms of assessment raise a number of issues for managers of education institutions, teachers and learners. These cover organizational as well as educational concerns. The political and educational context of the vocational curriculum reveals some recurring themes in the policy and practice of assessment which appear across the whole education and training system.

The following chapters each deal with a different aspect of assessment in the vocational curriculum, highlighting practical features, key terms and some of the educational or organizational dilemmas which assessment can raise.

In doing this, the book aims to:

• offer a practical guide to the technical features and activities involved in assessing learners achievements;

- provide some ideas about how teachers and managers of institutions can organize and use assessment more strategically;
- highlight some of the complex issues involved in carrying out assessment well.

Further reading

Reports, guidelines and technical advice

Capey, J (ed) (1995) *GNVQ Assessment Review: Final report of the review group*, NCVQ, London.

Further Education Funding Council (1995) *Assessment of vocational qualifications in the further education sector in England and Wales*, FEFC, Coventry.

Further Education Funding Council (1995) *General National Vocational Qualifications in the Further Education Sector in England*, FEFC, Coventry.

Further Education Development Agency (1995) *Managing Assessment*, FEDA, London.

Further Education Development Agency (1995) *Implementing GNVQs: A manual*, FEDA London.

Background issues

For practical insights, the following are useful.

Ecclestone, K (1994) *Understanding Assessment: a practical guide for teachers and managers in post-compulsory education*, NIACE, Leicester.

Further Education Development Agency (1995) *Assessment Issues in Further Education*, FEDA, London.

Rowntree, D (1987) *Assessing Students: how shall we know them?* Kogan Page, London.

For more detailed explorations of some of the issues, based on evidence from research, the following are useful.

Gipps, C (1995) *Beyond Testing: towards a theory of educational assessment*, Falmer Press, London.

Horton, T (1990) *Assessment Debates*, Hodder & Stoughton, London.

Torrance, H (ed) (1995) *Evaluating Authentic Assessment*, Open University Press, Buckingham.

2   Understanding Assessment

Many of the recent changes in the design and content of vocational qualifications signify an important educational and social shift from assessment which emphasized testing for the purpose of selection, towards assessment designed to enhance learners' ability to learn.

Assessment in the vocational curriculum serves a number of different purposes. The recent social and political commitment to raising levels of participation in learning programmes has led to new systems for accrediting achievements. Research findings suggest that good teaching incorporates assessment as a powerful motivator, by developing learners' abilities to assess their own learning and set targets for it. There is a growing body of evidence that diagnostic assessments, and in particular self-assessment, can foster a deep engagement with learning as opposed to a surface approach which emphasizes merely getting through the required processes of assessment (Gipps, 1995; Torrance, 1995).

A commitment to using assessment more positively has raised a wider awareness of what good teachers have always known – that bad assessment demotivates people, reduces their ability to engage with, and monitor, the success of their own learning. It also replaces the positive attributes of motivation and active learning with an instrumental commitment to overcoming a series of obstacles. There is now a widespread recognition that an over-emphasis on testing in the past has discouraged many people from continuing their education. Poorly designed assessment can also have an adverse effect on the way the curriculum is designed and taught. Much criticism has been levelled in the past – and is still expressed – at the distortion of learning and motivation which is caused by 'teaching to the test'. Torrance (1995) believes that assessment, particularly in traditional forms of testing, has often been used in the past as a 'threat', and as a basis for giving out educational and social rewards and penalties. As NVQs and GNVQs evolve, the tension between assessment for testing and assessment for promoting learning remains a central feature in debates about assessment in vocational qualifications.

This chapter aims to:

- outline reasons for assessing learners;
- highlight some of the main features of assessment;
- provide a framework for teachers, students and course designers in which to think about assessment and to plan for its different purposes.

Why we assess learners

For many teachers and learners the requirements of final assessment have an enormous impact on their perceptions about assessment and the range of methods used to do this. In some vocational courses, such as GNVQs, final assessment consists of aggregated grades from course work assignments, evidence of achievement in the elements of competence laid down by the awarding body, and externally set and marked tests. In others, such as NVQs, it is the accumulation of evidence to show that elements and units of competence have been achieved. It is not only teachers who view assessment as being primarily about final tests or marked assignments. Students, parents, prospective employers and admissions tutors at the next stage of progression also tend to focus on assessment, which certificates achievement and thereby provides a basis for selection in employment and in higher and further education. In the design and delivery of vocational qualifications, final assessment has played a dominant role.

The need to guide teachers and managers through the requirements of assessment has led to more prescriptive assessment regimes and an increasing reliance on guidelines issued by the NCVQ and awarding bodies. At the same time, there is a desire to use assessment to motivate learners and to diagnose their learning needs. GNVQs in particular have explicitly elevated the role that assessment can play in learning by highlighting the role of processes such as planning, review and self-assessment. In spite of this, the pull of final assessment is still extremely strong. It can reinforce a tendency to downplay other important purposes of assessment – to diagnose learners' initial needs and starting points, to assess their prior learning, to motivate them to chart their progress and achievements, to help them take an active role in their own learning.

There is strong evidence from research (Gipps 1994; Boud 1988) that when teachers are encouraged to consider a range of different purposes of assessment, they are more likely to use assessment more consciously in their teaching, and to draw on a wider range of assessment techniques. If this range of purposes is overlooked, there is a tendency to revert to simply assessing the performance of those tasks which seem most like the familiar, formal tests.

In thinking about assessment, it is helpful to consider:

Figure 2.1 *Questions to consider*

There are three main reasons for assessing learners, no matter what type of course or programme they are following:

- *to diagnose* their learning needs;
- *to select* them for the next educational stage or for work;
- *to certificate* their achievements.

Assessment carried out to meet each of these purposes provides information for different 'stakeholders' and interested parties in the education and training system. Each of these stakeholders has different interests in the outcomes of assessment and will require different information from them. More controversially, assessment is increasingly being used to compare the overall achievement of institutions and teachers through the publication of results for GCE A-levels and GCSEs. Assessment is therefore used at different times to provide information for a diverse range of stakeholders: government; funding bodies; awarding bodies; employers; higher and further education admission tutors; parents; learners.

Diagnosis

Assessment to diagnose learning provides information primarily for learners and teachers. It underpins the teaching and learning process by building on previous experiences and achievements gained before embarking on a programme. Assessment therefore aims to:

- provide a basis for negotiating individual starting points (for example in 'core skills' or determining preferred learning styles);
- diagnose an individual's needs and aspirations for the programme and for progression after it has finished;
- provide a basis for negotiating parts (or all) of a programme around a person's particular needs;

- motivate and enthuse learners by enabling them to see gaps in their learning, to see their achievements and strengths, and to identify new targets for learning;
- enable teachers and learners to make decisions about future possibilities for progression.

Important features of diagnosis include offering initial guidance, providing regular tutorial support and opportunities for learners to review their progress on a regular basis, using feedback from the teaching and learning process. When diagnostic assessment is carried out coherently across different programmes, it enables organizations to provide support on a more individualized basis for learning in areas such as literacy, numeracy and information technology. These features are discussed in more detail in Chapter 5.

Selection and recruitment

Although schools, colleges and universities have become much more flexible about their entry criteria, a process of assessing and selecting learners at the admissions stage is still used. It is still common for the criteria on which this assessment is based to be implicit rather than public.

Assessment is used by admissions tutors, employers, institutional managers and course designers to differentiate between learners in order to:

- *recruit* people to jobs by stipulating particular professional qualifications, NVQ units of competence, or required grades from an academic or vocational qualification;
- *admit* learners to learning programmes by publishing different entry requirements;
- *select* people to practice a trade or profession by requiring specific types of experiences or membership examinations.

Certificating achievements

Teachers, admissions tutors and employers use assessment to provide concrete evidence of learners' skills, competence and other achievements as a basis for progression into other learning programmes or employment. As more learners – particularly adults – progress from informal programmes outside education and training organizations into formal ones, certification and proof of achievement can make this progression easier.

The use of assessment to confirm achievement is open to public and political evaluation. It provides information for:

11

- *evaluation* of progress towards the NTETs;
- *funding* decisions based on retention and completion rates;
- *the presentation* of league tables;
- *debates* about rising or falling standards and about the relative merits of different types of learning programmes eg, vocational v academic.

Assessment is carried out on behalf of a range of interested parties in different sectors of the education and training system to achieve a range of purposes. Teachers, learners, institutional managers, admissions tutors, employers, funding councils, and the government all have an interest in the outcomes of assessment at different stages of a learning programme. Assessment can therefore answer a number of questions, shown in Figure 2.2.

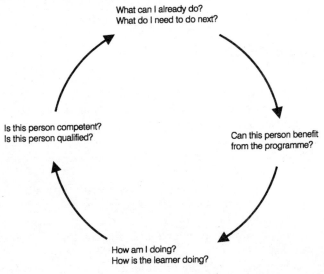

Figure 2.2 *Questions assessment can answer (adapted from Ecclestone, 1994)*

The purposes of assessment therefore fall into two main categories: *formative assessment* and *summative assessment*. Each has a set of activities associated with it which are carried out for different interested parties.

Formative assessment

Formative assessment is a powerful and often underestimated aid to learning. Diagnosis is the cornerstone of formative assessment and provides teachers with information which they can use as feedback to learners about strengths and weaknesses in their learning. When used well, the outcomes of formative assessment can provide learners with a powerful impetus to monitor and evaluate their own learning. Its outcomes provide information and feedback primarily for learners, but also for their teachers and tutors. It can be used to:

- guide and advise learners about the various opportunities, choices and possibilities open to them, either inside the school or college itself, or in other agencies;
- find out what a person's learning needs are at the beginning of the whole programme, or for different modules during it;
- draw up a learning plan, action plan or learning agreement;
- offer constructive written or oral feedback about someone's skills, knowledge or understanding;
- review progress and achievements in line with a learning agreement or action plan drawn up at the start of a programme;
- motivate learners to improve their own performance by becoming more reflective and able to monitor their own learning.

Formative assessment is therefore crucial for effective learning, and it is underpinned by notions of diagnosis and feedback in order to increase the effectiveness of learning. It is difficult to improve the quality of teaching and learning without it. (Chapter 5 deals with this in more detail and also expands on the points about good practice which are outlined below.)

Good practice in formative assessment
Teachers can greatly enhance the positive role of formative assessment when they:

- *clarify* how formative assessment can enhance learning;
- *explain* its timing, terminology, the role of staff, the purpose of feedback, the learner's own role in the process;
- *work collaboratively with learners* to clarify standards and criteria and to identify gaps in performance;
- *provide exemplars* of 'ideal' performance;
- *recognise and celebrate* a wide range of *achievements*.

Motivating people to learn, and to see assessment as a vital part of learning, is an essential part of formative assessment. It is carried out solely for learners and teachers, and the results or outcomes do not need to be open to public scrutiny.

Summative assessment

In contrast to formative assessment, the outcomes of summative assessment provide information which is publicly available for a number of external stakeholders or interested parties. Summative assessment is therefore associated with the public evaluation of 'quality'. Although learners need the information so that they can make decisions about progression, it is primarily carried out on behalf of admissions tutors, institution managers, employers and funding councils. It can be used to provide information for education and training organizations, employers and funding bodies which enables them to:

- make selection and entry decisions;
- give exemption from traditional entry requirements;
- infer someone's potential at the next level of employment, education or training;
- certificate (or accredit) someone's prior learning and achievements for all or part of a qualification;
- formally confirm achievement at the end of a learning programme or module;
- make decisions about funding;
- evaluate organizational and teachers' performance.

Good practice in summative assessment
This requires teachers and managers of institutions to:

- make consistent decisions and judgements about what constitutes adequate evidence, taking into account different types of evidence and different candidates;
- administer tests and make decisions about grading;
- interpret the guidelines and requirements from awarding bodies;
- discuss, agree and moderate the criteria used by colleagues for these;
- verify the consistency and quality of assessment decisions through the internal checking and moderation of standards.

Confusing formative and summative assessment
It is now common for vocational qualifications such as GNVQs to claim a central role for formative assessment, while at the same time requiring detailed processes for summative recording, testing and grading. This can create a tension between the time needed to carry out effective formative assessment and the time needed to meet the requirements of summative assessment. It is therefore easy to confuse the processes of formative and summative assessment.

Summative assessment is associated in many people's minds with examinations, tests and formal grades. Formative assessment tends to be associated with 'softer', more supportive methods, such as helping learners record their achievements or carrying out reviews of their learning. It is important to recognize that the different *methods* and *processes* used in assessment do not denote their formative or summative use. There is a wide range of assessment methods and processes and they can be used either formatively or summatively, depending on the reason for carrying out the assessment. All assessments have the potential to fulfil a summative function, whereas assessment is only formative if the feedback which learners get from it enables them to improve and change their performance.

In spite of the emphasis given to formative assessment in GNVQs, there is a danger that assessment can drift away from a careful and conscientious attempt by many teachers to diagnose learning needs, towards a fragmented and mechanistic process of compiling evidence towards what is needed for summative assessment. This can lead to a 'filling in gaps' approach, where formative assessment is used as a means of simply charting progress towards achieving all the requirements. This has also been a tendency in the National Curriculum.

It is therefore a common, but easy, error to confuse *continuous* assessment with *formative* assessment. Continuous assessment might merely be an ongoing process of accumulating evidence or grades towards a final assessment, in which case it is *continuous summative* assessment. Continuous assessment might, on the other hand, refer to the day to day, informal and formal assessments which teachers make about learners and their learning, and to their use of feedback to learners. In this case, it is part of *formative* assessment. Unless assessment provides feedback about learning and enables learners to become actively involved in this process, it is not playing this formative role.

What assessment is

Assessment is often seen as a formal or informal process of 'measurement'. There are common and crucial features in this measuring activity:

'It requires two things; evidence and a standard or scale. Evidence may take many forms from casual observation to extended technical tests or written examination papers. Standards or scales may take many forms but all involving measuring the individual against one of three things:

- *an absolute criterion* 'can this person add 2+2 to make 4?'
- *a cohort or group* 'can this person do this better than the average of the group/this year's candidates/all mathematicians?'

    — *the learner's own previous performance* "can this person do this better than they could last week/month?" (Ecclestone, 1994)

This attention to measurement, combined with attention to the summative purposes of assessment can lead to an excessive preoccupation with the technical aspects of assessment, such as grading, recording results, ticking off competences, administering assignments and tests. Many teachers find it difficult to associate the hundreds of informal assessments they make as part of the teaching and learning process every day with an act of 'measurement'.

From a broader point of view, all human interaction involves some sort of assessment and measuring process, and this may range from the most informal and incidental to the formal and technical processes we associate with summative assessment. Rowntree (1987) reminds us that an overlooked and important feature of assessment is that it is also 'an attempt to *know* a person. In this light, assessment can be seen as a human encounter'. It might, however, be useful to see assessment as an act of measurement on a continuum from an informal and open-ended process initiated by a teacher or by a learner, to a more prescriptive and formal one required by an external body. In this continuum, the standard or scale might be decided by the student, using his or her previous performance to design it, or it might be the 'absolute criteria' set by the awarding body used as a measure of progress. This continuum is illustrated below in Figure 2.3.

INFORMAL		FORMAL	
Learner designs his/her own criteria and targets	Teacher and learners use combination of student targets and externally set criteria to plan learning activities and review progress	Teachers use external criteria to review progress towards the accumulation of evidence	Teacher and awarding body use externally defined criteria to assess if learners have met requirements for certification
Tutorial/review	*Tutorial/review*	*Tutorial/review*	*Teacher marking*
Self-assessment	*Classroom activities. Questions and discussion*	*Teacher marking and assessment*	*Internal verification Verification by awarding body*
FORMATIVE DIAGNOSTIC	**FORMATIVE CONTINUOUS**	**SUMMATIVE CONTINUOUS**	**SUMMATIVE FINAL**

Figure 2.3 *From formative to summative assessment*

How we assess

Comparing learners

Formative and summative assessment both use some form of criteria or standards for measurement. These might be explicit and presented in public documents or explained by teachers, or they can be implicit and held in the minds of teachers and examiners and not communicated to learners. The criteria might be informal and negotiable between teachers and learners, or formal and prescribed by awarding bodies. Until the introduction of GCSEs, criteria for assessing performance were largely based on a process of *norm referencing*. These used *notions of how other 'excellent', 'average' or 'poor' learners perform*, (these notions are usually implicit in teachers' thinking and not made public), and *direct comparisons with other students* in the same group or annual cohort, or between cohorts over a period of time (as in the current debate about A-level standards).

Norm referencing therefore uses criteria arising from the norms of achievement set by other learners. It is a process which standardizes and ranks student performance in relation to the highest and lowest level of attainment shown by other candidates. Institutions, employers and awarding bodies often use it as a way of comparing one year's performance with that of previous cohorts in order to evaluate standards.

An individual's achievement is therefore measured in comparison to:

- *peers* from a learner's class or group;
- *a wider group* of candidates, such as the annual regional, local or national group undertaking the assessment;
- *historical data* from a particular cohort over a period of time.

Norm-referencing aims to:

- enable educational institutions and employers to *select* people when there is competition for limited places;
- allow teachers and examiners to *rank* learners in order of preference;
- enable external bodies to *compare the relative performance* of learners over a period of time.

Recent uses of assessment to open up wider access to learning opportunities and to motivate learners, mean that norm referencing is now widely seen to have negative educational and social effects. Criticisms arise from a number of features:

- Criteria for comparing learners are often based on *tacit or implicit* notions of what constitutes good or poor performance held by teachers and examiners.
- These criteria are *rarely shared* between teachers, examiners and learners, so that learners do not know how their performance will be judged.
- The actual level or *standard of achievement* for the top and the failure mark *varies each year* between different cohorts, resulting in a complex process of adjusting the distribution of marks.
- Information about *the grade and rank order dominates* teachers' and learners' perceptions about what is important in the learning process and down-plays the importance of individuals' achievements or how they gained them

There has therefore been a concerted move away from norm referencing towards the use of external measures or standards. In spite of this, there can be very strong pulls back towards norm referencing as a result of social, political and educational pressures. Disagreement about whether GNVQs are equivalent to A-levels, for example, is partly because GNVQs do not use norm-referenced grading, and the usual league table comparison is therefore difficult to make. Norm referencing can formally and informally affect assessment when:

- demand for access to places exceeds the number on offer or there is pressure on resources for selection and admissions processes;
- employers, parents and other interested groups wish quickly to compare standards of performance between learners through the use of league tables;
- *criteria for assessment are not debated* between teachers or shared between learners;
- *test designers use notions of a 'typical' learner* in setting tests and assessment tasks and teachers mark learners' work by setting the 'best' and 'worst' standard in the group for high and low marks;
- *teachers use notions of 'high' and 'low' ability* when describing learners and the quality of their work.

Using external measures

The history of the vocational curriculum shows that there has been a concerted attempt to base assessment on explicit statements of intended learning outcomes and criteria for measuring them. These have been introduced in order to counteract some of the effects of norm-referenced assessment. The influence of NVQs and GNVQs has been particularly strong in this respect. *Criterion referencing* aims to remove the negative effects of ordering learners by rank and comparing them with others from the assessment process.

Criterion referencing therefore compares someone's performance with externally defined and explicit criteria, which aim to tell the assessor and the learner what level, range and type of performance is expected. It intends to:

- provide the basis for *specific and detailed information* about what someone can actually do and what they have achieved;
- *describe the requirements* for assessment and any grading which might take place so that they are more easily understood by learners, teachers and assessors;
- provide a basis for *objectively evaluating the curriculum* and the teaching and learning processes which underpin it;
- enable assessors and awarding bodies to *verify judgements* made about learners using the same publicly available criteria;
- make it easier for learners to *seek accreditation* of achievements gained outside formal learning programmes by relating them to explicit standards.

The growth in the educational and political popularity of criterion referencing has arisen from different social and educational trends which are all closely connected. First, there is a political and educational consensus that the education system plays a crucial role in raising levels of skill and achievement in employment. This links to a view that employment and a licence to practise in different occupations should be based on clearer and more detailed descriptions of what people can actually do. If this is the case, the scant information about grades and rank orders which have traditionally been provided, is no longer adequate.

Second, if people are to be motivated to participate more and achieve at higher levels, access to education and training should be based on much more explicit and extensive definitions of what constitutes achievement. In turn, these definitions should be based on clear criteria and standards. Third, if learners are going to be motivated to achieve, these criteria should be at the forefront of the learning process so that learners are able to take more control of their own learning.

Setting personal targets and measures

In contrast to externally defined measures of norms and criteria for assessing pre-determined outcomes, *ipsative* (self-referenced) assessment provides learners with a personalised form of criterion referencing. This has been widely used in the past in adult and community education and in programmes for learners with special learning needs. It has recently received growing attention in other curriculum areas.

Ipsative assessment measures learners' performance against their own previous performance and targets, using criteria which they have set for themselves. It is therefore different from *self-assessment*, which is often carried out by learners against criteria given to them by a teacher or an awarding body. It can be used in conjunction with other approaches since the process of ipsative assessment builds up confidence and the skills of self-assessment before learners move onto measurement against externally defined standards.

Ipsative assessment is most effective when:

- *learners are motivated to set their own targets* and monitor their progress against them;
- *there is no external requirement* to assess learners against a pre-defined standard;
- *learners want to be actively involved* in becoming independent and autonomous learners.

Figure 2.4 summarizes the purposes, timing and features of assessment at different stages in a learning programme.

Technical features of assessment

Examining and awarding bodies, educational researchers and institutions have traditionally devoted much time, money and effort to improving the technical design and implementation of assessment. Although it is commonplace for examining and awarding bodies to pass on this expertise in the form of guidance to managers and teachers in schools and colleges, it is extremely useful for teachers to consider how they and their colleagues deal with the technical features of assessment in their own formative and summative practice. This section provides a brief overview of the two main features which underpin current forms of assessment in the vocational curriculum: *reliability* and *validity*.

Until the introduction of criterion-based systems, assessment was heavily influenced by the development of testing – and particularly psychometric testing – which aimed to predict ability and intelligence, and to present learners' achievements in rank order. Since learners' progression to restricted opportunities at the next stage has traditionally rested on this, the *reliability of grades* was a paramount consideration. It was important to aim for *consistency* of results between assessors or between the outcomes of the same test used with different groups of learners.

PURPOSE OF ASSESSMENT	TYPE	FEATURES	TIMING	STAFF	EXTERNAL REQUIREMENT
INITIAL GUIDANCE – assess someone's prior learning – diagnose starting points and individual needs	Formative Criterion-referenced Self-referenced	Criteria may be set by: – awarding body – institution – individual learner	Before a whole programme. At the beginning of a module within a programme.	Course leader. Guidance or careers adviser. Module leader. Personal tutor. Admissions officer.	FEFC: impartial guidance and information, opportunities for assessment of prior learning and diagnostic assessment. NVQs: opportunities for APL (accreditation of prior learning).
ADMISSIONS – give exemption from entry requirements – make decision about entry and potential to benefit from programme – make decision about eligibility to seek APL	Summative Should be criterion-referenced (although pressure for places can lead to re-emergence of norm-referencing)	Criteria set by: – institution – awarding body – NCVQ – professional body	After some initial guidance. Before a programme or module starts.	Admissions tutor. Course leader.	NCVQ: removal of unnecessary barriers for entry to NVQs. Provision for APL in NVQs.
IN-PROGRAMME – diagnose needs and targets – record/observe progress – record evidence for: • grades • achievement of competences	Formative Criterion-referenced: external and self-referenced Summative (ongoing) Criterion-referenced, but possible tendency for comparison between learners to bring in informal norm referencing	Tutorials Self-assessment Peer assessment Teacher assessment Tests/assignments	Regularly, during classroom and workshop activities, and in planned tutorials/reviews. During modules. End of a module. End of programme.	Tutor/teachers from core and subject areas. Subject teachers. Course leader. Internal verifiers.	FEFC and GNVQs: report progress regularly, opportunities for review. Student charter: some colleges and universities have set specific targets for marking, return times, quality of feedback.
CERTIFICATION – confirm achievement	Summative	Accumulation of grades from ongoing summative assessment. Certificates References	After modules or whole programme.	Subject teachers. Course leader. External verifiers.	NCVQ: facility for unit certification. GNVQ: mandatory external tests and facility for unit certification.

Figure 2.4 Purposes and timing of assessments

In contrast, the technical features of assessment in the vocational curriculum have been heavily influenced by a relatively recent drive for assessment methods and associated criteria which can accurately assess a wide range of abilities, skills and attributes. *Validity* requires assessment methods to enable assessors to make accurate *inferences* about learners' achievements. Valid assessment should therefore measure the learning outcomes it claims to measure.

The drive to increase validity has led to specifications of learning outcomes and criteria which are as understandable as possible. It is believed that the technical accuracy of these specifications will lead to consistency and reliability of assessors' judgements. However, the technicalities of both reliability and validity are extremely complex and there is much overlap between them.

Reliability

Where assessment fulfils a summative purpose, great emphasis is placed on a method's reliability. Norm referencing in particular, with its function of limiting access to a restricted number of places in employment or education, has played an important role in promoting reliability. The notion of reliability therefore stems from the need for an assessment to:

- reproduce the same range of results in a different set of learners who are deemed to have similar abilities;
- differentiate between the best and worst performances which might be expected from a particular cohort;
- produce agreement and consistency amongst assessors about the relative quality of a student's performance.

Designing an assessment based on reliability
Test designers use a number of complex statistical and design features, and this area is complex. However, the main features of assessments based on reliability include:

- measuring one underlying attribute in a particular test item, based on the predicted norms of the cohort being tested;
- standardizing test administration, tasks and scoring with an emphasis on their amenability to be measured statistically;
- not allowing testers to be involved with the learners' performance.

Institutions and awarding bodies attempt to ensure reliability and to offset inconsistencies in assessment by different assessors by using a number of mechanisms. These include:

- Analytical marking schemes to ensure that assessors award a specific number of marks for particular features in a student's work.
- Averaging grades over several examination papers marked by different assessors.
- Moderation and sampling of papers by internal and external assessors.

An assessment for *summative purposes*, that uses norm referencing, therefore places a strong emphasis on reliability.

Validity

Criticism of the limiting social and educational effects of norm-referenced assessment, and an interest from the 1960s onwards in assessment for 'educational' purposes, led to the development of criterion-referenced testing. This is premised on a belief that assessment systems should accurately assess individuals' achievements rather than compare the performance of different cohorts. Assessment should also be able to identify strengths and weaknesses as a means of promoting progression and achievement.

The introduction of NVQs and GNVQs, and forerunners such as the Certificate of Pre-Vocational Education, was accompanied by claims about the merits of extending the range of outcomes which should and could be assessed, and the need to make sure that assessment really did measure what it claimed to measure. Criterion-referenced assessment places a strong emphasis on validity. NVQs and GNVQs place great emphasis on increasing the validity of assessment. This requires a much greater degree of teacher assessment as opposed to the design and administration of examinations by awarding bodies. Valid assessment enables different interested groups to be sure that they can depend on interpretations of learners' performance, and upon inferences of their future ability to apply knowledge or skills again. Valid assessment therefore aims to enable test designers and assessors to:

- infer as accurately as possible that learners can apply a skill or knowledge in another assessment situation and in the future;
- reach similar judgements and interpretations to those of other assessors about what is being assessed and why;
- present public descriptions of the purpose, scope and methods of assessment which 'match' the type of learning outcome they are assessing;
- use a range of appropriate methods which can measure different skills, knowledge and attitudes, and which assess a much wider range of skills, knowledge and attributes than assessment has traditionally aimed to do.

Designing a test based on validity
Test designers and assessors must identify:

- the test's specific purpose and what it will indicate about a particular skill or attribute;
- how it will be used and by whom;
- what the specification of the test should encompass whilst keeping it inside manageable boundaries;
- expectations about the quantity and quality of evidence on which assessment will be based.

Awarding bodies, managers of institutions, and teachers attempt to ensure validity by establishing procedures for standardizing assessors' decisions in line with the criteria. Processes for *internal and external verification* can therefore:

- *clarify expectations* about standards, quality and quantity of evidence;
- *cross-moderate* colleagues' assessment decisions and discuss the basis for these, between different subject areas and across different centres, as well as in one particular programme;
- *develop exemplars* of good quality work and discuss their implications for the quality and level of work expected from learners.

Debates about the relative value of assessment reliability or validity, can – like debates about formative and summative assessment – be traced back to wider questions about assessment's social functions. These create tensions between selection and the desire for wider access; between the technical implications for assessment of focusing on a broad range of achievements and the narrower, more easily assessed achievements of paper-based examinations. Current forms of assessment have also raised issues about the balance between teachers' professional judgements and their accountability to specifications from awarding bodies.

Summary

It is possible to differentiate between assessment carried out for formative and summative purposes. This shows that formative assessment in particular has a central role in diagnosing learners' needs and in helping them to be more effective as independent learners. However, the demands for summative assessment are still very strong and there can be a danger that formative assessment becomes subservient to them. It can be helpful for teachers to also differentiate between norm- and criterion-referenced assessment, and to recognize the strong pulls towards norm referencing. Notions of validity and reliability can help managers and teachers to identify their effects on methods of assessment as well as their crucial role in the internal and external verification of assessment standards and judgements.

Further reading

Practical guidelines
Ecclestone, K (1994) *Understanding Assessment*, NIACE, Leicester.
Further Education Unit (1994) *Implementing GNVQs*, FEU, London.

Background issues
For the rationale behind the introduction of NVQs and GNVQs and their particular model of assessment.

Burke, J (ed) (1995) *Outcomes, Learning and the Curriculum: implications for NVQs, GNVQs and other qualifications*, Falmer Press, London.
Jessup, G (1990) *Outcomes: the emerging model of education and training*, Falmer Press, London.
Rowntree, D (1987) *Assessing Students: how shall we know them?* Kogan Page, London.

For an examination of the history and academic research background which has informed changes to assessment practice.

Boud, D (1988) *Developing Student Autonomy in Learning*, Kogan Page, London.
Gipps, C (1994) *Beyond Testing: towards a theory of educational assessment*, Falmer Press, London.
Torrance, H (1995) *Evaluating Authentic Assessment*, Open University Press, Buckingham.

3 Assessment in Vocational Qualifications

The introduction of National Vocational Qualifications (NVQs) and General National Vocational Qualifications (GNVQs) has been given a very high political profile. This is the latest manifestation of a general shift throughout the education and training system towards a vocationally oriented curriculum. The history of the vocational curriculum in schools and colleges over the past 15 years shows that the assessment systems used in NVQs and GNVQs have their origins in various government initiatives from the late 1970s onward, such as the Technical Vocational and Education Initiative, introduced in 1982, and the Certificate of Pre-Vocational Education, introduced in 1984. Different initiatives emanated from separate branches of government – the Department of Education and Science, the Department for Education, the Employment Department and the Training and Enterprise Councils, and the Department for Education and Employment. A number of common themes in how assessment is designed and organized in the vocational curriculum can be traced through these initiatives, and are now manifested in debates about wider access to learning opportunities and the educational and political role of assessment in NVQs and GNVQs. They are similar to debates about assessment in the National Curriculum and higher education.

Current qualifications and assessment systems in the vocational curriculum aim to fulfil a range of educational and social purposes. These attempt to ameliorate the negative effects which have tended to characterize traditional forms of assessment. Assessment, therefore, has to perform a number of functions, not all of which are compatible with each other.

First, it has to provide various interested parties with detailed and valid accounts of learners' achievements which go beyond the rather limited information provided by grades. This gives better information to higher and further education institutions and employers about what learners have achieved and what they can do as a result.

Second, if new qualifications are to attract different and wider groups of learners, assessment has to be able to motivate them to want to learn and to be effective assessors of their own learning. To do this, assessment has to diagnose the causes of success and failure in learning in order to spur learners on to greater achievements!

Lastly, the recent history of assessment throughout the entire education and training system shows the increasing importance which is being attached to evaluating and assuring the quality of learning programmes, and of providing funding bodies and government with evidence that qualifications are accessible, accountable and efficient.

This chapter aims to:

- define the scope of the current vocational curriculum;
- identify the roots of NVQs and GNVQs in different vocational initiatives;
- identify the main assessment themes which have been emerging in the vocational curriculum since the 1970s.

Defining the vocational curriculum

Terms like 'vocational', 'academic', and 'general' are fraught with complex and controversial meanings and different concepts of 'curriculum' arise from the emphasis given to each of these notions. Defining what the vocational curriculum encompasses is therefore not straightforward. Different traditions, educational aims and values are embodied in notions of the 'vocational' curriculum, just as they are in notions about the 'academic' curriculum. Yet the concept of the vocational curriculum has strengthened its influence over the whole education and training system, in the same way that assessment has. It has become a central tenet of policy making for all sectors of the system and in public debate about the purposes of education and training.

Preparing people for general employment or specific occupations has always been seen by many as a crucial purpose of education and training. Schools, universities and colleges therefore prepare their pupils and students for employment with varying degrees of specificity or generality in the various learning programmes and qualifications they offer. However, it is by no means agreed that this is education's main purpose, and there have always been fierce debates about how far learning should be related to the needs of employers or the economy.

Nonetheless, the defining characteristic of debate about the wider purposes of the education and training system as a whole over the past 15 years, has been the consensus that high levels of participation and achievement are inextricably linked to national and economic prosperity. Vocational preparation and job-related training now enjoy an unprecedented ascendancy throughout the education and training system, and this is reflected in the introduction of GNVQs into schools and colleges, and their likely extension into vocational degree programmes in universities. In spite of this, the relationship and balance between the 'vocational' curriculum and 'general', 'liberal' and 'academic' education remain controversial and contestable (Pring, 1995).

In defining the scope of the vocational curriculum, a broad spectrum, from direct job training to the most general development of skills and attributes which employers might want, shows that all education and training can be described as 'vocational'. Figure 3.1 shows this spectrum of definitions.

Preparation for employment in a subject discipline, especially for university or industry research	Vocational preparation of professionals, planned specifically for a group in the labour market and offering them job-specific skills and practice	General overview of an occupational area with a set of skills, qualities and knowledge valuable to employers	Fortuitous preparation, where students make connections between what they are studying and the labour market
A-level courses degrees Masters' degrees	**NVQs professional qualifications short training courses**	**GNVQs HNDs vocational degrees**	**academic courses non-vocational courses adult education courses**

Figure 3.1 *Vocational programmes (based on Silver and Brennan, 1988)*

From this broad spectrum, A levels and Philosophy degrees immediately cross the academic/vocational divide! For the purposes of this book, however, vocational is taken to have an *explicit employment-related* focus. This might take one or more of the following forms:

- An introduction or overview of a particular occupational area which introduces learners to the scope and activities of an area, such as GNVQs, Higher National Diplomas and degree programmes related to occupational areas.
- Specific skills training for a particular job role, such as NVQs and employer-specific programmes offered by a college or university or a training organization
- A combination of both, such as GNVQs or degrees, combined with some units of competence from an NVQ, or a Higher National Diploma.

- There are also many professional development programmes which cover both 'initial' training and continuing professional development.

Different vocational programmes and qualifications require learners to demonstrate different levels and balances of skills, knowledge, personal attributes and qualities. The range of what is encompassed in the vocational curriculum is therefore extremely wide. Until the advent of GNVQs a distinction was made between 'pre-vocational' and 'vocational'. Pre-vocational tended to emphasize a broad view of skills and knowledge related to general employability, while 'vocational' reflected closer links to a particular occupational area. This distinction is no longer made. Recently the vocational curriculum has been also strongly influenced by different traditions and expectations about assessment.

For both new and experienced teachers, getting to grips with assessment in the vocational curriculum can be quite confusing. It is becoming more common for teachers to have to work with different assessment systems such as a competence-based 'pass/fail' one, and one where grading or even norm-referenced comparisons are used. This is particularly true in universities, but is also true for those who teach and assess both A-levels and GNVQs, or a combination of these with NVQs. The contexts where teachers might assess the vocational curriculum have increased over the past five years to include sixth form colleges, further education and tertiary colleges, adult and community providers, universities and colleges of higher education and, increasingly, the workplace itself.

The changing vocational curriculum

Different political, social and educational ideas appear throughout the history of assessment, and particularly in the evolution of the vocational curriculum which has been emerging and changing for over 100 years. The vocational curriculum does not, therefore, have one single, coherent history or a defining set of characteristics. Features of NVQs and GNVQs have some of their origins in different traditions stretching back to the 19th century, such as the development of specific craft skills or employer demands that people should be 'employable' on leaving education and training. Other features come from developments in criterion-referenced assessment from the 1960s, and still others – such as an emphasis on student-centred learning and accreditation of prior learning – have their roots in adult education. In relation to assessment, its *current* forms and principles reflect the various interests of those bodies who shape qualifications, assessment systems and learning programmes.

Different groups and bodies

The range of bodies and groups who have shaped the evolution of the vocational curriculum is wide and – in spite of the rationalization of vocational qualifications undertaken by the NCVQ – still extremely confusing to an observer. There are over 150 examining and awarding bodies and over 1700 qualifications.

'Historically, there has been no national body to control the setting up of examining and awarding bodies in England. As new professions and crafts have developed, new training and qualification routes have been created in a piecemeal fashion. There is consequently a wide range of organizations able to offer qualifications… The development of different bodies reflects distinct traditions in craft and apprenticeship training, in academic and general vocational education and in professional development and recruitment.' (Nasta,1994).

The range of bodies involved in the design and implementation of qualifications includes:

- *Awarding bodies and examining bodies* such as:
    - the Business and Technology Education Council (BTEC);
    - the City and Guilds of London Institute (CGLI);
    - the RSA Examinations Board (formerly linked to the Royal Society of Arts, Commerce and Manufacture, but now a completely independent examining board);
    - London Chamber of Commerce and Industry Examinations Board (LCCIEB);
    - GCE A-level examining boards;
    - individual universities which validate their own degrees as well as short courses for employers and other organizations.
- *Membership bodies* such as trade unions and chambers of commerce.
- *Professional bodies and associations*, many of which offer qualifications and NVQs, sometimes in conjunction with awarding bodies such as CGLI, BTEC and universities.
- *The NCVQ* which accredits awarding bodies to offer the standards of occupational competence developed by *lead bodies* in qualifications (NCVQ is not an awarding body itself – it accredits other bodies to award NVQs based on occupational standards).
- *Lead bodies* consisting of employers' and employees' representatives who undertake the initial 'mapping' of an occupational area and then a detailed functional analysis of all the roles in this area. These become the standards of competence used by *awarding bodies* to propose qualifications for accreditation by the NCVQ.

- *The National Open College Network (NOCN)* which accredits programmes in adult and community education.

Education and training providers

A large number of organizations can now be validated – ie given formal approval – to provide vocational programmes and to assess and accredit learners' achievements. These include:

- universities;
- further education and sixth form colleges;
- school sixth forms;
- training organizations and employment training schemes;
- adult and community education organizations (eg, the Worker's Education Association);
- prisons;
- employers.

An evolving vocational curriculum

The history of the pre-vocational and the vocational curriculum since the 1970s is characterized by a series of government-funded initiatives, developed and implemented by the different bodies above, with different traditions and approaches to assessment. These initiatives are summarized below. They also relate strongly to other changes in schools and colleges, particularly the piloting of *records of achievement*.

Technical and Vocational Education Initiative (TVEI)

This was set up and funded by the Employment Department under the direction of the then Manpower Services Commission. Funding has been given since 1982 and is due to finish in 1997

Aims
To develop vocationally-oriented learning opportunities for young people aged 14–18 in schools and colleges across the whole ability range. These opportunities were intended to supplement rather than replace other parts of the curriculum.

Features
- Schools and colleges have developed work and community placements.
- Curriculum aims emphasize a broad pre-vocational preparation for work

and leisure, including personal, social and health education.
- A strong emphasis is placed on the processes of guidance, counselling and formative assessment.
- Records of achievement provide a focus for learners to review their progress and achievements.
- A summative statement of competencies and skills gained is compiled at the point of learners' progression into something else, and it combines the learner's own statements with those of a teacher or tutor.

Certificate of Pre-Vocational Education (CPVE)

This was set up in 1984 by the then Department for Education and Science and jointly accredited by the Business and Technology Education Council (BTEC) and the City and Guilds of London Institute (CGLI). It was replaced in 1988 by the Diploma of Vocational Education.

Aims
To provide a certificated programme of broad vocational preparation for young people aged 16–19 in schools and colleges, and to encourage those who might otherwise have left school to stay on. It was intended to cover the whole ability range in school sixth forms and colleges, and to supplement other programmes, such as GCE A-levels. In practice, it tended to become part of provision for learners with 'special educational needs' in many colleges, although it had a broader target group in a large number of schools.

Features
- Colleges and schools worked together in consortia to provide a wide range of modules.
- Learners were encouraged to sample a range of vocational and general occupational areas during the programme.
- A strong emphasis was placed on personal tutorials and reviews, formative assessment and guidance and counselling.
- Schools and colleges developed work and community placements, links with employers and other local organizations.
- Assignments had a practical and work-based focus, covering vocational competencies and a range of core skills in problem solving, numeracy, communications, personal and career development, information technology. They enabled learners to gains specific skills in a vocational areas and to explore the functions and activities of different occupational areas.
- Learners compiled evidence of achievement for these competencies and other areas identified by them in records of achievement, drawn from regular reviews of progress and targets for learning.

- Learners and teachers jointly produced a summative statement of achievement which listed units gained during the programme and included an extensive statement of core skills and other achievements.

Employment training schemes

Training initiatives and schemes for unemployed young people and adults
A variety of initiatives have been set up by the Employment Department through the MSC (which has changed its title and remit several times) since 1978. These are now administered through the Training and Enterprise Councils (TECs) in England and the Local Enterprise Councils (LECs) in Scotland.

Aims
To provide work experience, job training and life and social skills to unemployed young people and adults.

Features
- These began with little or no formal assessment and emphasized a combination of work experience and job training, as well as providing training in job seeking and other life and social skills.
- Trainees had work placements, either with employers or on community-based training schemes.
- Work experience and on-the-job training was supplemented with college and other forms of off-the-job- training, such as life and social skills.
- Certification of off-and on-the-job training has increased since 1986 and is now done largely through NVQs, particularly at levels 1 and 2.
- Funding by the TECs to education and training organizations is increasingly based on recruitment and 'outputs' of NVQ units gained by trainees.

Vocational qualifications

Qualifications awarded by the Technician Education Council (TEC), the Business Education Council (now BTEC – the Business and Technology Education Council), the City and Guilds of London Institute, the Royal Society of Arts (now RSA Examinations Board), the London Chamber of Commerce and Industry Examination Board.

Aims
Before the introduction of NVQs, a diverse range of bodies offered qualifications across a large number of vocational areas, and levels of study from

basic job-related training to professional level qualifications. Many have been rationalized into the NVQ framework, and BTEC National and Higher National Diplomas have partly been incorporated into the emerging GNVQ framework. However, there is still a significant number of qualifications outside the NVQ system, such as the qualifications offered by professional bodies.

Features
- Different awarding bodies have based their formal assessment and certification on different combinations of examinations and tests, course work and assignments, grading or a pass/fail system. Each awarding body has therefore evolved its own system of assessment and accreditation
- A wide range of occupations and levels is covered by the main awarding bodies, and some awarding bodies offer certification for customized employer-based training, such as that provided by Sainsbury's supermarket chain and British Airways.
- Many universities validate and certificate local employer-based training as part of vocational degree programmes.

National Vocational Qualifications (NVQs)

NVQs were introduced by the National Council for Vocational Qualifications in 1986. NVQs are based on standards of competence developed through occupational lead bodies which are set up and administered by the Employment Department (now merged with the Department for Education). These standards are the basis for qualifications accredited as NVQs by the NCVQ.

Aims
To rationalize the vast array of vocational awards offered by diverse bodies, and to provide a framework of job related training covering all occupational areas and functions. NVQs aim to establish national standards of competence across all occupational areas. They are primarily designed for people in work who need to accredit the competencies they have already gained and to move into new areas of occupational skill. They are also extensively used for training students and unemployed young people and adults.

Features
- A detailed functional analysis of a particular occupational area describes the different roles and functions and the area's 'key purpose'. These roles and functions determine the scope of activities the standards of competence cover and the performance criteria to assess them.

- Elements of competence are disaggregated from this initial functional analysis. These elements form units of competence each representing a discrete role or function. Individual units of competence can be accredited separately so that learners can accumulate them over a period of time.
- NVQs are offered at five different levels which range from routine and supervised activities, to work which involves a high degree of autonomy, planning and responsibility for the work of others.
- Assessment is based on performance evidence from normal work settings, from simulated work activities and from past experience and achievements at work, and in other areas such as home management, voluntary and community work etc.
- Assessment is based upon the demonstration of evidence of achievement in elements and units of competence, using a pass/not yet competent form of continuous assessment.
- Learners compile evidence of achievement in portfolios and submit this for assessment, as well as demonstrating competence through tests and questioning.
- NVQs are intended to give learners opportunities to gain credits from previous learning: Accreditation of Prior Learning (APL).
- Assessment is not linked to learning programmes, duration or particular experiences and 'the mode of assessment should not place unnecessary additional demands which may inhibit or prevent a candidate from showing what they know or understand' (NCVQ, 1994)

Figure 3.2 shows the structure and scope of assessment in NVQs.

General National Vocational Qualifications (GNVQs)

These were introduced by the Department for Education in 1991, and implemented by the NCVQ in 1992. GNVQs are offered by BTEC, City and Guilds and RSA. They are aimed at full-time students in colleges and schools to provide a coherent framework of general vocational preparation at three levels: foundation, intermediate and advanced. At advanced level, they are intended to offer a recognized alternative to the GCE A-level. There are proposals to extend GNVQs to higher education. The outcomes, performance criteria and grading system for existing GNVQs are designed by the NCVQ and the three awarding bodies.

Aims
To provide a vocational alternative to GCE A-levels and to provide a broad preparation for an occupational area at different levels, either for progression into employment or further and higher education.

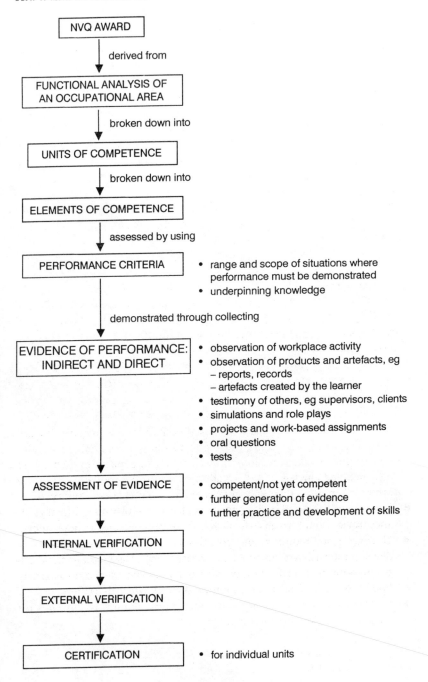

Figure 3.2 Assessment and accreditation in NVQs

Features

- GNVQs consist of individual units specified in the form of learning outcomes to be achieved. There are *mandatory* and *optional* units which cover vocational areas and core skills. These must be integrated into the teaching and assessment of GNVQs. There are three *mandatory core skills* units in Communication, Application of Number and Information Technology. These are set at increasing levels of difficulty and each GNVQ incorporates core skills units at the appropriate level. Other core skills are offered as *additional units* – 'Working with others' and 'Improving own learning and performance'.

- GNVQs are offered at *three levels*, from Key Stage 4 of the National Curriculum to equivalence with 2 GCE A-levels. *Foundation* level consists of six vocational units and three core skills units at Level 1, and is usually offered as a one year programme for post-16 learners who are not yet ready for an Intermediate GNVQ. *Intermediate* level consists of six vocational units and three core skills units at Level 2. It is designed to be of comparable standard to four GCSEs at grades A* to C and is usually offered to post-16 learners in a one year programme. *Advanced* GNVQ is designed to be of comparable standard to 2 GCE A-levels. It consists of twelve vocational units and three core skills units at Level 3, and is usually offered to post-16 learners over two years. There are proposals to extend these to vocational degree programmes in universities.

- *Assessment* is based on the *achievement of specified outcomes* in the units, accumulated throughout the programme in a *portfolio of evidence*. Grades of merit and distinction are given for evidence of learners' ability to plan their work, to seek and handle information and to evaluate their work critically, demonstrated in evidence from the portfolio. There are also *external tests* of underpinning knowledge and understanding which are designed and administered by each of the awarding bodies, and which can be taken more than once if learners do not pass them the first time.

- Strong emphasis is placed on processes for action planning, initial guidance, review and formative feedback about progress and achievements.

- GNVQs place requirements on schools, colleges and universities to develop internal systems to ensure consistency of assessment standards through internal verification of assessors' judgements, and on awarding bodies to check standards through visits from external verifiers.

- *Certification* can be given for individual units. Figure 3.3 outlines the structure of assessment in GNVQs.

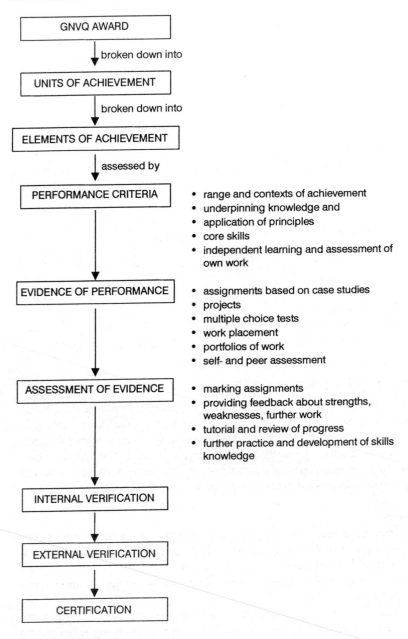

Figure 3.3 Assessment in GNVQs

Modern apprenticeships

These were introduced by the Department for Employment in 1995, organized through partnerships between employers and Training and Enterprise Councils (TECs). Modern apprenticeships offer training at craft, technician and junior management level.

Aims
To enable young people to gain work-based training and qualifications at NVQ level 3 or above, along with core skills determined by each occupational sector.

Features
- Assessment is based on the NVQ system (see pp.53–56).
- Modern apprenticeships are aimed at 16-17 year old school-leavers, with selection criteria drawn up by employers and Industry Training Organizations according to the needs of each occupational sector.
- Employers are expected to contribute to the costs of training and/or wages, and supply job supervision.
- Young people receive a training allowance, although employers are encouraged to employ them for the duration of the apprenticeship.

Vocational degrees

Universities can validate and award their own degrees and validate specific employer-related training programmes. The post-1992 universities (ex-polytechnics) have developed a diversity of occupationally-related degrees, as well as training for entry into certain professions. Accountancy, law, computing studies, nursing and teaching are just some of the areas covered by vocationally-related degree programmes.

Features
- Increasing numbers of degrees and programmes for employers are designed as part of a *modular* system, where learners can accumulate credits in flexible combinations towards a degree.
- The amount of academic, work-based and on-the-job training varies with each programme.
- Validation procedures to approve or review a degree involve employers, professional associations and potential learners closely in the design and approval processes.
- Assessment is still heavily influenced by norm referencing to arrive at degree classifications, but it increasingly involves criterion-referenced and competence-based assessment as well.

Figure 3.4 Assessment in Vocational Qualifications

		ASSESSMENT IN VOCATIONAL QUALIFICATIONS			
MAIN FEATURES	**LEVELS**	**TYPES OF ASSESSMENT**	**SCOPE OF ASSESSMENT**	**PURPOSE**	**PARTICULAR FEATURES**
General National Vocational Qualifications General overview of an occupational area – its roles and functions in the economy and society as a whole, its scope and employment opportunities. 1995: Business, Health and Social Care, Leisure and Tourism, Manufacturing, Art and Design. By 1997: Science Construction, Hospitality and Catering, Information Technology, Hand-based Industries, Media and Communications, Management.	Foundation. Intermediate. Advanced, with proposals (1995) to extend into degree programmes.	External tests for underpinning knowledge. Projects and assignments for application of knowledge and evaluation. Grades of merit and 'distinction' for evidence of planning, evaluation and monitoring the quality of own work.	Core skills: Communication, I.T., Application of Number, problem-solving, monitoring and improving own work. Working independently. Propositional knowledge. Application of knowledge.	Diagnosing initial needs in core skills. Action planning and target setting. Formative and diagnostic review and assessment of progress. Summative accumulation of evidence, against performance criteria in a portfolio.	Unit accreditation. Mandatory and option units for core skills. Extensive assessments, specifications and requirements. Systems required for internal verification in schools and colleges.
National Vocational Qualifications Job and occupation – specific skills and functions, covering 90% of all occupational areas by 1997. Accredited by over 70 awarding bodies. Based on functional analysis of the key purpose of an occupational area, broken down into functions and tasks.	Five levels from routine, supervised work to work with a high degree of autonomy and responsibility for the work of others.	Units of competence, composed of elements of competence. Detailed performance criteria for range and scope of performance, the types of evidence and underpinning knowledge. Emphasis on work-based assessment.	Functions and tasks in a job role, comprising task management, working with others.	Diagnosing prior achievement and 'gaps' in evidence. Formative assessment focuses on 'gaps' in evidence. Summative accumulation of evidence from past and current achievements.	Unit accreditation. Accreditation of Prior Learning. Extensive assessment specifications and requirements. Systems required for internal verification. Workplace assessors.

MAIN FEATURES	LEVELS	TYPES OF ASSESSMENT	SCOPE OF ASSESSMENT	PURPOSE	PARTICULAR FEATURES
Higher National Diploma Offered in colleges and universities in a large number of vocational areas, often as the first year of a degree. Awarded by BTEC and may be replaced by GNVQ Level 4.	Aimed a supervisory/ management level. Forms part of degree programme.	Continuous formative and summative assessment. Criterion referenced.	Propositional knowledge, application of knowledge to practice, evaluation. 'Common' skills (some similar to core skills in GNVQs). Work experience.	Emphasis of summative accumulation of evidence.	Proposals to use GNVQ Level 4.
Degree Introduction/overview of vocational area with some job- or occupation-specific skills. A very wide range, including all the areas covered by GNVQs, with additional areas of nursing, teacher education, social work, youth work, law, accountancy, economics. Some professional qualifications form part of a degree, but can be accredited separately at different exit points, eg Certificate, Diploma. Some universities accredit work-based learning and in-house staff development towards degree credits.	From year 1 of an undergraduate programme to Masters. Levels 1, 2, 3 and M in the higher education CAT (Credit Accumulation and Transfer) scheme based on progression through the yearly stages of a degree.	Strong traditional emphasis on norm referencing to arrive at degree classifications. Many universities are adopting criterion referenced assessment. Emphasis in some professional programmes on portfolios of evidence and 'reflective' journals or logs.	Propositional knowledge. Evaluation, synthesis and analysis. Research skills. Professional reflection. Awareness of occupation in wider social and political context.	Strong emphasis in the past on summative assessment for ordering degree results by rank. Growing use of diagnostic and formative assessment, and peer and self assessment.	Internal procedures for validating, reviewing and monitoring programmes. Internal moderation. External moderation. There can be a tension between norm- and criterion-referenced assessment.
Masters degree In addition to degrees in academic subjects, there is a growing range of programmes in professional subjects with a strong emphasis in some areas on action research into aspects of professional practice or policy.	Some programmes are designed in discrete stages with credits attached to each exit point, eg Certificate and Diploma.	As for degree.	Analysis and evaluation of professional roles and contexts. Professional reflection and insights. Research methods.	As for degree	As for degree

Common assessment themes

GNVQs have derived their assessment regime from their pre-vocational and vocational predecessors, particularly the CPVE. They have also been heavily influenced by the impact of the NVQ assessment system. A number of themes are therefore discernible throughout the history of different initiatives, which affect the focus of assessment and systems for implementing it. These themes reflect changes in the emphasis given to different aspects of assessment.

> General education ⟶ vocational preparation
> Knowledge recall ⟶ doing and understanding

The growing influence of general vocational preparation and work-based learning has affected the design, content and assessment of the vocational curriculum at all levels. Core skills in GNVQs and in some A-level and NVQ programmes, have an explicitly vocational focus.

Assessment increasingly requires learners to demonstrate a wide range of practical skills, cognitive abilities and personal qualities, rather than skills in recalling propositional knowledge.

> System centred ⟶ learner centred
> Report ⟶ record

Assessment systems have become more flexible and sensitive to the needs of individual learners. They place learners more firmly at the centre of assessment. The principle of open access to assessment is applied, which means that it should be available to all those who have the potential to meet the standard. Evidence of achievement and its assessment and accreditation is explicitly separated from a prescribed time scale, location or type of learning programme. This gives learners more opportunities for gaining credits for individual units or modules, and for seeking credit for achievements which might have been gained at work or in other life experiences.

In place of brief reports, teachers' judgements are presented through examples of evidence presented in more detailed records.

> Normative ⟶ criterion-referenced and ipsative

Assessment systems and specifications are based on criterion referencing in the form of competencies, performance criteria and the range of situations, knowledge and understanding which must be covered. This has replaced norm referencing as the main form of assessment. It also denotes a shift towards much more extensive and prescriptive specifications designed by awarding bodies and which teachers and learners have to interpret.

Passive learner ——————⟶ active learner
Extrinsic ——————⟶ intrinsic

There is an increasing emphasis on learners taking more responsibility for their own learning by setting targets and assessing their own performance. Colleges, schools and universities are increasingly offering opportunities for initial guidance, diagnostic assessment and regular reviews of progress and achievement. Records and portfolios of evidence of achievement are now extensively used in these formative processes and for summatively confirming that requirements have been met.

Post-mortem ——————⟶ diagnosis
Negative feedback ——————⟶ positive feedback

Instead of retrospective judgements about someone's performance based on 'terminal' assessments, assessment now emphasizes collaboration between learners and teachers in making judgements, agreeing evidence and recording achievements. The need to use assessment in more motivating ways has shifted the focus from judgements about how well or badly learners' performance compares with that of other learners, to better feedback about strengths and a more informed diagnosis of weaknesses.

Organizational implications

Although these themes have been emerging over a period of time, it has not been common for organizations to build upon the implications of each initiative as it was introduced. A 'piecemeal' approach to each initiative and its requirements for assessment has been compounded by the involvement of different branches of government, different educational traditions and the confusing array of awarding bodies' diverse practices and requirements. This can make it difficult for organizations to respond strategically to the assessment issues which developments in the vocational curriculum have presented.

There are organizational implications in managing these issues. The introduction of NVQs and GNVQs, with proposals to extend these into higher education programmes, affects the way that assessment is organized and managed. Greater expectations of what assessment can measure and how it can influence teaching and learning, mean that the processes to administer it are becoming more technically complex. Teachers and learners have to interpret detailed specifications of the range of learning outcomes and competencies which must be covered and the criteria which must be used to assess and accredit them. Although there is now a great deal of similarity between awarding bodies in their terminology and procedures, assessment specifications have presented difficulties for teachers and awarding body verifiers in managing a large volume of assessment judgements and a wide range of evidence. Huge amounts of advice and guidance are currently emanating from awarding bodies, the NCVQ, the FEFC Inspectorate, the Further Education Development Agency (FEDA) and the Schools' Curriculum and Assessment Authority (SCAA) in an attempt to help educational institutions deal with the NCVQ's and awarding bodies' requirements for assessment.

Summary

Existing vocational qualifications have their origins in a history of various pre-vocational and vocational initiatives over the past 15 years. These initiatives have promoted a powerful and positive role for assessment in both curriculum design and in the way that teachers carry out assessment. Assessment methods and processes in NVQs and GNVQs are, in many ways, the logical outcome of different systems tried out in earlier pre-vocational and vocational initiatives. There has been a much greater political impetus behind the introduction of NVQs and GNVQs: they are intended to rationalize the vast array of qualifications offered and to provide vocational preparation which has parity of esteem with 'academic' qualifications. Most importantly for colleges, schools and universities, their assessment requirements are more detailed and prescriptive, with many features still being amended as problems are found in their implementation. This makes it important for teachers and managers to have an understanding of the origins of assessment and to adopt a strategic approach to dealing with their implications.

Further reading

Practical guidelines/information
Ecclestone, K (1993) *Understanding Accreditation: ways of formally recognizing achievement*, FEU, London.
Further Education Unit (1992) *Towards a framework for curriculum entitlement*, FEU, London.
Hayward, G (1995) *Getting to Grips with GNVQs; A Manual for Teachers*, Kogan Page, London.
National Council for Vocation Qualifications (1994) *NVQ Criteria and Procedures*, NCVQ, London.
Nasta, T (1994) *How to Design a Vocational Curriculum*, Kogan Page London.

Background issues

For an analysis of changes to the design and purposes of the curriculum, including the vocational curriculum, and some of the debates which have accompanied them:

Pring, R (1995) *Closing the Gap: Liberal education and vocational preparation*, Hodder & Stoughton, London.

Silver, H and Brennan, J (1988) *A Liberal Vocationalism*, Methuen, London.

Wolf, A (1995) *Competence based assessment*, Open University Press, Buckingham.

4 Assessment in a Modular Curriculum

Single subject, linear courses where each learning activity and every aspect of the content are compulsory for all learners are becoming a thing of the past. Profound changes to the way the vocational curriculum is designed and organized have accompanied the shifts in assessment charted in this book. Assessment is increasingly based on descriptions of the learning outcomes that can be gained and performance criteria to assess them. Programmes are increasingly designed around smaller 'units' or 'modules', and have produced a growth in systems for credit accumulation and transfer. These enable learners to accumulate credits for units, putting together different combinations according to the requirements of a particular qualification, and to negotiate more individualized programmes of study. Modular, credit-based programmes can potentially be much more flexible than traditional courses where learners start a programme at the beginning of an academic year and finish at the end of the following one. Many programmes have option modules as well as requirements for core or mandatory modules. In some cases, learners can combine parts of general or academic programmes with specific vocational or core units, for example GCE A-level units with GNVQ units. In some programmes, it does not matter which order modules are taken in, in others there might be restrictions about modules that must be taken first.

The history of the vocational curriculum shows that the legacy of diverse arrangements for accreditation between different awarding bodies has led to 'a fragmented curriculum with few opportunities for students to move between the course-based qualifications offered by the major validating bodies' (Nasta, 1994). This means that learners' choice is still predominantly 'between one course of study or another and not one of accumulating chosen modules which can be employed for a range of different learning and assessment purposes' (Nasta, 1994). The evolution of different traditions in the design, implementation and assessment of the vocational curriculum means that there is also a confusing array of terminology and structures in different modular systems.

Modular programmes raise particular management issues in planning and implementing assessment and accreditation of prior learning, offering initial guidance and diagnostic assessment and providing tutorial support across programmes which might be drawn from different curriculum and subject areas. Information and administrative systems are needed for tracking individual learners' progress and achievements, and for certificating individual modules or units. If the potential flexibility of modular programmes is to be realized while maintaining coherence in assessment and learning experiences, colleges, schools and universities have to incorporate these features into an assessment strategy.

This chapter aims to:

- describe the main features of a modular curriculum;
- show how assessment and accreditation of prior learning fit into a modular curriculum;
- outline some implications of a modular curriculum for assessment.

Different modular systems

Credit-based systems

There are currently five main systems that enable learners to take individual units or modules which can be accredited separately. Learners therefore gain credits for achievement of individual modules and can accumulate these over a period of time. In some cases, credits can be transferred to other institutions and other programmes. These include:

- *University and higher education* Credit Accumulation and Transfer system (CATs), where credits are based on the four levels of a three year degree programme and one year for a Masters' degree.
- *The Open University* where learners work towards credits through distance learning, based on the levels of degree and Masters' programmes.
- *The post-16 credit framework* being developed by the Further Education Development Agency (FEDA), which aims to provide a framework of credit-rated units of learning within which other credit systems can operate.
- *National Vocational Qualifications* (NVQs) and *General National Vocational Qualifications* (GNVQs) where individual units of competence in NVQs and vocational and core units in GNVQs can be accredited individually.
- *National Open College Network* (NOCN), which aims to accredit adult and community education in vocational and non-vocational subjects in credit-rated units.

Each of these systems has evolved separately and there is still a great deal of disparity between terminology and levels used. FEDA's work on a post-16 credit framework aims to create common understandings about terminology and features of modular curricula based on credit accumulation and transfer. There is growing interest in regional arrangements between universities, further education colleges and adult education providers, where a broad credit framework is provided within which different accreditation systems can operate. However, the technical issues are complex and research and development work is still to be done on harmonizing different modular and credit-based systems.

Non-credit based systems

Some programmes are designed in modules to enable greater choice and flexibility in what is studied, but credit is given for the final award rather than for individual modules or units. Some modular degrees fall into this category.

Different modular structures

Subject-specific linear systems
In this type of system, all modules which make up a programme and/or qualification are based in one subject area and presented in a linear sequence. The order in which a learner takes the sequence of modules may or may not be prescribed. Each module is assessed separately and there may be opportunities to accumulate credits for each one over a flexible period of time. If this opportunity is not provided, the programme is modular in design but not credit based.

Subject-specific systems with options
Modules are linked to a particular subject area, but there may be opportunities for optional modules outside those which are compulsory. Different structures are possible: introductory or foundation modules might be compulsory; there might be a choice of core modules, and a more open choice of option modules.

Combined approach
A modular programme might cross different disciplines while remaining in a broad subject area, and include core modules from one main subject area with option modules from other, related subjects. The title of the final qualification might depend on the option modules which someone has chosen to study, or it could relate to the subjects covered by the compulsory modules.

Cross-curricular approach

If an organization's entire provision is modularized and credit based, learners can combine quite different modules. There may be specific requirements for a particular qualification, such as a module in 'problem solving' or 'study skills', or subject-specific core modules. Other cross-curricular programmes offer pathways through different modules in a broad subject area. Combined degree programmes often enable a large degree of flexibility for putting together different combinations of core and optional modules across different subject areas.

Features of a modular curriculum

Most modular systems have common features, although terminology and structures within each system vary. A number of features below are explored in this chapter:

- modules and units;
- learning outcomes;
- assessment criteria;
- credits;
- levels;
- quality assurance;
- recording systems.

These features are common to all modular curricula, although individual institutions will be at different stages in developing them. However, there is wide variation in how terms are used and the way in which information is presented. The allocation of credit to modules or units can vary considerably, as does the notion of 'level' on which definitions of learning outcomes and progression to the next stage is based. The development of different qualifications by different awarding bodies has given rise to a proliferation of terms related to the specification, design and assessment of modular-based systems.

Modules

Defining what a module represents in different modular schemes is not straightforward, and the term itself is often used interchangeably with 'unit': people might therefore refer to 'unitized' or 'modularized' programmes. 'Module' might refer to a module for assessment and credit rating purposes, or to a module of learning. It might be a self-contained set of learning outcomes, with clearly defined assessment criteria which can stand alone and be taken in isolation from other modules. It can also refer to individual parts of an overall syllabus of knowledge and skills which has been simply divided into periods of study, in which case it is still part of a holistic curriculum.

In GNVQs and NVQs, modules are discrete sets of learning outcomes, with performance criteria and details of the range and scope of learning. In higher education, degree and Masters' programmes, modules might be little more than smaller parts of the syllabus, or they might be part of very sophisticated systems where individual learners can combine diverse subjects and activities into an entire degree.

In an attempt to promote some consistency between terms and structures of different credit-based systems, FEDA has differentiated between modules and units by referring to a *module* as an *aspect of delivery and part of a learning programme*, so that modules can be different sizes. A *unit* is a *coherent set of learning outcomes, assessment criteria* and is *credit rated*. In this definition, learners gain credits for the successful completion of units. The learning outcomes of a unit might be achieved through one module or through a number of modules.

Learning outcomes

Many experienced teachers have been trained to use *aims* and *objectives*. Some might differentiate more finely between *general* objectives, *specific* objectives and *principal* objectives. In the National Curriculum, teachers refer to *statements of attainment* and *attainment targets*. In GNVQs, *elements* define skills, knowledge and understanding to be assessed. NVQs consist of *elements of competence* and *units of competence*.

There is therefore no agreed single definition of, or common language to describe, learning outcomes across different sectors of the education and training system, or different subject traditions and curriculum areas. Some qualifications express learning outcomes in very broad terms of 'indicative content' to be covered. In contrast, others use very comprehensive specifications of behavioural outcomes which are assessed in conjunction with detailed performance criteria. The umbrella 'learning outcomes' is helpful for encompassing all these different terms.

The term 'learning outcome' encompasses what it is that a learner can do, what she or he knows or understands, and what personal qualities and attributes he or she might have as a result of a learning process. Learning outcomes can be expressed very broadly and generally, or be extremely specific and detailed. They cover a diverse range of areas, including:

- *Personal skills and qualities*: study skills, mental characteristics (such as agility, creativity), integrity, initiative, emotional resilience, ambition, empathy.
- *Interpersonal skills and qualities*: team and group work, problem solving, communication.
- *Knowledge*: propositional and factual, situational, about people, practices in jobs or professional areas, processes and how to get things done.
- *Skills*: practical and technological, communication, organizational, social, and cognitive skills such as synthesis, evaluation and analysis.

Learning outcomes which make up individual modules and whole qualifications can cover a wide range of different learning processes and activities. It is important in designing modular programmes to ensure that there is a balance of different types of learning outcomes covered by the overall combination of modules. Assessment methods therefore have to be matched to these so that they are appropriate and valid for different types of learning outcome. (For further discussion of assessing different types of learning outcomes see Chapter 7.)

Purpose of learning outcomes
FEDA outlines the current prominence of learning outcomes throughout the education system as follows:

- The need to *ensure consistency of interpretation* in order to underpin reliable national standards.
- *The movement towards more learner centred programmes* and assessment, and the associated need for transparency and clarity in planning learning.
- *Increased emphasis on valid and reliable assessment*, and therefore clearer identification of the measurable outcomes of learning.
- *The need for effective tools for curriculum and staff development.*
- *Increased emphasis on public accountability* and the accompanying need to measure achievement reliably.

(FEDA, 1995a)

Assessment criteria

Criteria are external definitions of the standard and quality of evidence which learners must demonstrate in order to achieve learning outcomes. They should include indications of the required standard and scope of performance. They might be referred to as *assessment criteria* or *performance criteria*.

Criteria normally contain information about the standards of perform-ance, and any progression, such as the level of autonomy required from learners, the complexity of the task and the range of contexts where it should be demonstrated. Criteria are usually written in statements which specify an *action verb, content and qualifiers*. Qualifiers describe requirements for com-plexity, the degree of independence and autonomy required and the range of contexts. The example below is based on FEDA (1995).

Learning outcome
Apply market theory to a specific case study

Assessment criteria
Express a real resource problem in terms of relative supply and demand
Suggest credible ways of implementing solutions, covering most major possibilities
Evaluate possible solutions in terms of their impact on the problem and on producers and customers

There may be further specifications outlining the qualifiers described above. Adjectives, such as 'critical', 'accurate' or 'appropriate', usually need further examples which more precisely define the range and scope of these criteria in the particular context of a module, at a certain level, and in a certain subject area. In GNVQs and NVQs, these qualifiers can be quite extensive, provid-ing teachers with detailed 'evidence indicators' and descriptions of the required range. In other programmes, the criteria can be brief, relying heavily on teachers' own interpretations.

Written specifications on their own cannot adequately convey the re-quired standard or quality. The extensive specifications in NVQs and GNVQs illustrate the difficulties of trying to make the quality of desirable performance clear. Communicating the meaning of criteria to learners, and between colleagues, relies in the best specification possible within the constraints of language. It also needs to be supplemented by discussion between teachers, processes for moderation and the development of exem-plars drawn from learners' work, which give real examples of how criteria are interpreted.

Credits

Credit rating enables programmes to be designed in units of a standard size, so that each one carries a specific number of credits.

Credit is the *value* given to a unit of learning, based on the learning outcomes and level covered by the unit. Credit therefore carries notions of 'currency' and 'transferability', so that learners can accumulate credits over a period of time and then exchange them for parts of a qualification.

Credits can be used to establish an equivalence between different qualifications. Credits gained in units from one qualification may count towards units in another. In a degree programme, for example, credits have to be accumulated at three levels – 120 at level one, 120 at level two and 120 at level 3 – before a degree can be awarded. Learners can use relevant achievements from life and work experience to claim credits at a particular level, and universities that operate a credit system will consider this. (See later section on accreditation of prior learning in this chapter.)

Once the notion of credit is introduced, decisions about the level of achievement become critical because qualifications are usually described as being at a certain level.

Levels

The *level* of units, modules or whole qualifications is closely linked to credit rating. It is a complex and confusing area in the vocational curriculum because different subjects, accreditation systems and sectors in the education and training system, all use the notion of level in various ways. Outside the specific context where level is used, it can be difficult for employers, learners and teachers to understand how levels in different programmes relate to each other.

A description of level is often attached to the final qualification, such as an 'NVQ Level 3' or a 'GNVQ Level 3'. Broad equivalence between qualifications is now commonplace. People therefore refer to a GNVQ Level 3 as 'equivalent' to two GCE A-levels, or a Level 4 NVQ as 'equivalent' to a degree. This belies the complexity of levels which are based often on very different types of learning outcomes and criteria. Different interpretations of level arise from the various traditions in different qualifications and subject areas. Levels are difficult for teachers and learners to make sense of unless they are socialized into how they are interpreted in a particular system. The level of units in a modular programme, or given to a qualification, are usually based on different factors, such as those listed below:

- *A stage of development*, often related to expected and typical behaviours at certain ages (the criteria for assigning national curriculum levels are partly based on ideas about what a typical 11-year-old might be expected to achieve in mathematics, for example).
- *A hierarchical standard of achievement* based on criteria such as autonomy, independent learning, originality (the first two are the basis for GNVQ grades and a combination of these forms part of the criteria for degree classifications).
- *A time-based stage*; eg the three levels of a university CAT system are partly based on the three year time scale of a typical undergraduate degree and

the one year of a full-time Masters' degree. Other notions such as 'autonomy in learning', 'originality' or 'synthesis between theory and practice' might determine the learning outcomes in a module and its placing at a particular level.

- *The amount of autonomy* in an occupational role, and *responsibility* for the work of others (these are the underpinning criteria on which levels in NVQs are based).

Some subjects, such as science and languages, may need one unifying and coherent notion of level and progression through the subject. This might mean that progression has to be based on particular modules taken as pre-requisites or co-requisites. It might be easier in other subjects to mix up the order of modules since progression does not depend on the sequence of learning outcomes. In order to provide some coherence in programmes where the aim is to combine units or modules from different qualifications, designers and assessors of modular programmes have to consider the implicit criteria which affect the levels attached to units or whole qualifications. A number of strategies can help. These include:

- Careful definitions of learning outcomes and assessment criteria which try to capture a relevant and appropriate notion of level and which take account of likely combinations of modules.
- The use of assessment exemplars which show achievement at different levels and which make explicit the criteria which might have been used to decide the level of achievement.
- Discussion of the necessary modules which form pre-requisites or co-requisites in certain subjects or at different stages in a programme.

The chart in Figure 4.1 represents the way that 'equivalences' between qualifications are portrayed.

Quality assurance

Modular programmes need administrative procedures and information technology systems which can track learners' progress and achievements and ensure common mechanisms for recording learners' successful achievement of modules, accumulation of credit, and whether this credit has been transferred from another institution or programme. Procedures to validate, review and assure the quality of modular programmes are also important.

If learners are to have greater flexibility in progressing between different modular systems, some harmonization of terms is desirable, as well as an understanding of how different terms are applied in different systems. This makes it easier for learners to present their achievements to organizations

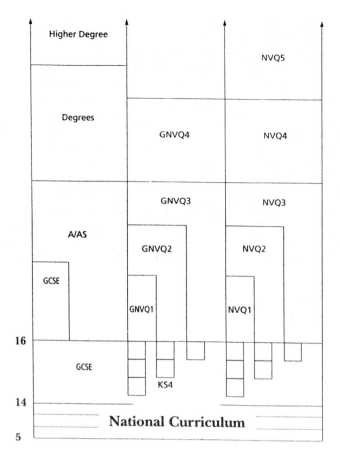

Figure 4.1 *Equivalences and levels in vocational qualifications (Reproduced with permission from* How to Design a Vocational Curriculum, *Tony Nasta (1994), published by Kogan Page*

for assessment and accreditation of their prior learning. There are other features to ensure the quality of assessment which are particularly important in modular programmes. These include:

- *Written specifications* of learning outcomes, assessment criteria, and descriptions of level, which take account of the appropriate basis for assigning a level.
- *Exemplars* are important for generating a common view of achievement at various levels in a modular curriculum. They are important for staff development and in quality assurance procedures. They can include what a module might cover, how it might be taught, typical examples of

an assessment plan, a programme or scheme of work, samples of learners' work (both good and poor quality) and examiners' and moderators' reports.

- *Networking and procedures for moderating assessment decisions* enable teachers, assessors and curriculum managers to arrive at better common understandings of learning outcomes, and interpretations of assessment criteria. These processes reinforce the information and understanding generated by having effective documentation and exemplars. Professional contact should be made between those who write modules, assessors and teachers, external examiners and awarding body verifiers.

Recording systems

Each module and each learner's programme in a modular and credit-based system is a discrete feature of a modular curriculum. Information and tracking systems therefore have the dual role of creating an assessment system for individual modules and for learners. This shifts the emphasis from tracking cohorts and whole courses. Such a degree of flexibility is still rare and the more flexibility there is for learners, the greater the administrative demands on the organization. Systems have to track learners' accumulation of credits towards accreditation and provide an up-to-date basis for awarding credits in separate units or modules.

Recording and information systems also need to provide qualitative and quantitative data for evaluating learners' achievements and monitoring the effectiveness of different programmes. They need to provide information for assessment boards, which discuss assessment decisions and track learners' choices for combining modules and their progress through them. More detail about procedures for quality assurance is provided in Chapter 9.)

Assessment and accreditation of prior learning

Assessing and accrediting evidence of achievement from a person's past work or life experience has been the focus of growing interest over the past five years, although its origins lie in adult education both here and in the United States. Providing more people with access to assessment and accreditation means that the skills, knowledge and insights gained from work and life experience are seen as valid evidence towards the learning outcomes in a formal qualification.

The process of assessing someone's prior learning and achievements has long been a feature of good teaching and admissions procedures, although it has only recently been given a formal title. The diagnostic and formative function of using what someone has already achieved, in order to help them identify their starting points for new learning, is crucial in ensuring that a learning programme is suited to their needs and aspirations. Many teachers informally, or more formally, assess learners' prior learning in order to establish their starting points at the beginning of a programme or module. Increasing numbers of schools, colleges and universities offer opportunities for learners to discuss what they can already do with someone in a guidance role, to help them decide what is best for them to do next.

A more formal and rigorous process of giving credit for someone's prior learning and achievement towards all or part of a qualification is, however, a relatively new feature of assessment and accreditation. The Access to Assessment Initiative, funded by the Employment Department, stimulated interest in developing services to provide APL. This enabled Training and Enterprise Councils to work with colleges and employers to enable people to gain NVQ units of competence based on evidence of achievement from life and work experiences, and to identify further training needs. As a result, more colleges offer a service for accreditation of prior learning, mainly for NVQs, but increasingly for other programmes too. APL is still rare in schools. In a large number of universities, schemes for credit accumulation and transfer (CAT) have been a spur to establishing formal systems for APL towards degree programmes.

Before the recent growth in formal procedures for APL, many institutions often made informal agreements to give people exemption from the usual entry requirements, or allow them to miss out part of a learning programme which they might have covered elsewhere. A new emphasis on APL has made more teachers and managers of organizations put proper procedures in place, which can formally recognize and accredit learners' previous achievements.

It is apparent that processes for assessing and accrediting prior learning are a source of some confusion among teachers, managers and learners. As a result, the acronym APL may describe processes for guidance and diagnostic assessment before a programme, or at the beginning of a new module.It might also denote a more formal process where learners submit their prior achievements for summative assessment, leading to accreditation. APL is often seen as a different form of assessment, which seems to require different procedures from those in other programmes. If the processes of assessing and accrediting prior learning are viewed as part of a range of assessment 'services' in a modular and flexible curriculum, APL can become a standard feature in all learners' assessment.

Principles of APL

Accreditation of prior learning is based on principles which have been a recurring theme throughout this book: widening access to learning and assessment opportunities, and using assessment in a positive way in order to motivate new groups of learners. It is therefore seen to have a number of benefits:

- It enables learners to see that 'achievement' can arise from formal and informal opportunities for learning and that they do not need to repeat learning, and assessment when they already have relevant knowledge and practical skills.
- It promotes the idea of lifelong learning by widening access to learning and broadening people's perceptions about where and how learning takes place.
- It explicitly commits education and training institutions to widening access to their programmes and to be more flexible about what constitutes appropriate experience for joining programmes.
- It enables institutions to offer a curriculum which is flexible, where there are opportunities to accumulate credits and transfer them to other learning programmes, and which enables learners to record and present evidence of their learning.

Challis points out that:

'The fundamental principle underpinning the Accreditation of Prior (Experiential) Learning is that learning is worthy and capable of gaining recognition and credit, regardless of the time, place and context in which it has been achieved. It thus represents a move to accept that learning is not dependent on any formal setting, and to acknowledge it as being of value in its own right' (Challis, 1993)

Accreditation of prior learning can therefore take different forms:

- The outcomes from acquired prior *experiential* learning (APEL) can be matched to the outcomes which can be gained through a formal qualification, and learners can seek 'credit' for these by showing how their learning matches that of the qualification.
- The outcomes from prior *certificated* learning can also be matched to outcomes in a formal qualification, often to gain exemption from a particular module or modules in a programme, or as an alternative to the usual entry qualifications needed to join a programme ('advanced standing').

Both of these sources of evidence can be put forward for formal certification and credits.

APL as part of a modular curriculum

A great deal of evidence put forward for assessment can draw on past achievements, as well as from current abilities assessed through conventional methods. Consideration of the processes which someone seeking assessment and accreditation of prior learning requires, enables an organization to view these as necessary for all learners. Initial guidance, selection, in-programme assessment and certification therefore apply in the same way to learners wishing to gain accreditation of their prior learning, as it does to learners following a conventional learning programme. The difference for someone seeking accreditation of prior learning is that their learning programme for individual units or modules primarily consists of compiling evidence from past achievements to meet the learning outcomes and assessment criteria. It is rare for past achievements to form the basis of accreditation for an entire qualification.

Accreditation of prior certificated learning

A learner may have gained qualifications or units from another institution. A college or university has to decide whether this counts for *general* or *specific* credit towards a particular qualification.

General credit enables an organization to decide if previous certificated study is at an appropriately similar level to that of the programme the learner wishes to gain access to. General credit is often used to give exemption from other entry qualifications, and the time scale in which the previous qualification was gained may not be especially important.

Specific credit is awarded for directly relevant or equivalent qualifications, where learning outcomes can be shown to match quite easily. This can enable learners to gain actual credits towards a qualification on the same basis as those following the programme that leads to it. For example, in some universities, someone with a City and Guilds Further and Adult Education Teaching Certificate (the 7307) can gain a specific number of credits against the first year of the Certificate in Education, thereby speeding up their entry into the second year of the Certificate.

Considerations for offering both general and specific credit will cover:

- the *age* of the qualification;
- what the *learning outcomes cover* compared to the one for which the learner is seeking credit;
- a *comprehensive tariff* of equivalent and relevant qualifications, including work-based training courses where an in-house certificate might be given or other locally designed qualifications which an organization agrees to give credits for;

- consideration of criteria for the *level of learning* in order to establish the equivalence of other qualifications.

Accreditation of prior experential learning

Generating the right sort of evidence to show how *experiential* learning meets the learning outcomes of a qualification, or individual modules or units, is more complex and more time consuming than systems for accrediting prior certificated learning.

Evidence is usually generated from *direct* and *indirect* sources. Learners normally assemble this evidence in a portfolio, and it might be supplemented with evidence gained from other assessment methods, such as question and answer or practical tests.

Direct evidence
This includes:

- *examples of work* – reports, memos, videos of someone at work, actual artefacts they have made etc;
- *certificates* from courses attended;
- *written explanations* of how learning gained elsewhere meets the criteria of the learning outcomes for which accreditation is being sought.

Indirect evidence
This includes *testimonials* from employers, colleagues, clients.

An assessor has to decide whether direct and indirect evidence is:

- *authentic* and genuinely the learner's own work;
- *current* enough to be able to infer that the person can still do what they say they can;
- *transferable* so that the person can do the relevant work but in a different context;
- *valid* and meets the range and scope of learning outcomes for which accreditation is being sought;
- *sufficient* in quantity, depth and comprehensiveness.

These criteria for judging evidence are no different from those assessors use to judge learners with whom they have been working during a traditional learning programme.

Identifying and documenting prior learning can be a discrete module in learning programmes and learners can gain credits for the process of doing this. Some colleges and universities offer programmes such as 'Making your experience count', which are sometimes accredited in access and university foundation programmes.

Figure 4.2 *Processes in APL*

Different types of assessment in a modular curriculum

In order to provide more opportunities for learners to negotiate their own learning programmes, an organization has to consider a range of assessment processes at different stages. These are outlined below and are based on the purposes and stages of assessment outlined in Chapter 2. The summary of assessment processes is based on Ecclestone (1994).

Initial guidance

Initial guidance has to cover a wide range of learners' needs.

At this stage learners are seeking:

- assessment to help them establish a career direction;

- assessment to enable them to recognize aptitudes and abilities;
- review and assessment of what they have learned from previous experiences;
- advice about whether they might be eligible for gaining accreditation of prior learning, and about how it relates to other ways of gaining all or part of a qualification, eg 'traditional' attendance on a programme, or more flexible methods, eg self-study and open learning.

Potential candidates for accreditation of prior learning are seeking guidance and advice about the possibility of APL, what they have to do and whether they are likely to be eligible to seek accreditation based on what they have done in the past. They may have very clear ideas about what accreditation they wish to gain using previous learning, or they may have no idea at all. They might be offering evidence of achievement from previous certificated learning, or from experience which has not been certificated – experiential learning.

To provide appropriate guidance, an organization has to have certain aspects of its provision clearly documented. It also needs to have access to different information, with clearly identified staff who can be called on for further advice if necessary. Access to a range of diagnostic tests is also important.

An organization has to provide:

- details of modules, assessment, accreditation and progression routes, with acceptable alternative routes and referral contacts in the organization or in others;
- a tariff of how other comparable qualifications can be credited with those offered by an institution, eg a good pass in GCSE Information Processing might equal credit for a GNVQ Level 2 core unit in Information Technology, or a local employer-based training course designed in conjunction with a university might count for a number of credits in a university's CATs scheme;
- details of pre-and co-requisites for individual modules, ie what must be accredited before a particular module, or which modules must be taken together;
- details of desirable or essential previous experience which are seen as important for different programmes, and the types and levels of particular skills and specialist knowledge;
- jargon-free information about the benefits of APL, with realistic information about how a learner might use it, details of costs, timing and expected workload;
- access to guidance and information in non-traditional settings, eg employers, community centres, adult education centres, libraries;

- a bank of diagnostic assessments and other activities for assessing prior learning and providing guidance.

Staff who need to be involved include:

- someone in a guidance role: external agency, eg careers service, TEC or in a college, school or university;
- admissions tutor in a college or university;
- general APL advisor;
- workplace advisor.

Assessment techniques and methods include:

- personal guidance interview;
- careers interest guides;
- self assessment exercises;
- opportunities to try out different skills;
- initial diagnostic assessment;
- workshops for compiling general portfolios of experience.

Entry decision

Many decisions about whether a learner can benefit from a programme are made from application forms, letters and references. They often do not involve a face-to-face interview. For learners who are making an application to join a learning programme, or to gain accreditation of prior learning, paper-based decisions are not the most appropriate way to make entry decisions.

At this stage, learners are seeking:

- entry to learning programme without having the traditional entry qualifications stipulated by the organization;
- a formal decision about whether they are eligible to gain accreditation for all or part of a programme through accreditation of prior learning.

To provide access to programmes using a wider set of criteria than the number of A-level points or GNVQ grades, an organization has to have access to information for making an entry decision.

The organization has to provide:

- guidelines about processes for APL from awarding bodies and particular subject areas in the institution;

- a list of certificated exemptions and alternatives which the organization will accept in place of the usual stipulated entry requirements;
- details of modules, how they can be combined, and any restrictions, eg some modules may require learners to take part in particular processes of learning, or take certain modules as pre- and co-requisites.

Staff who need to be involved include:

- general APL adviser;
- programme leader;
- admissions staff.

Assessment techniques and methods include:

- selection interview;
- examination of references, portfolios of evidence of prior learning;
- examination of any recommendations from pre-entry guidance and assessment.

Learning programme

For learners who are able to collect evidence from past achievements towards accreditation, all or part of their learning programme will consist of them working alone, or perhaps with other learners, to collect and present the necessary evidence.

At this stage, learners are seeking:

- opportunities to review and discuss progress;
- diagnosis of further needs and targets, and assessment to identify gaps in evidence;
- advice about sources for materials, self-study activities.

In providing the right procedures to help learners seeking APL, an organization has to provide assessment which can help all learners. This encourages teachers to see past and current achievements as valid sources of assessment.

An organization has to provide:

- details of where evidence is likely come from, examples of suitable experiences and sources of evidence;
- details of assessment criteria covering the scope and range of what is required from learners, evidence of knowledge, the range and scope of necessary contexts, and situations where learners must be able to perform;

- an assessment plan, showing opportunities for submitting evidence, a learning action plan and tutorial support for review and guidance;
- access to flexible and open learning assignments;
- regular opportunities for formal assessment, with good quality feedback from teachers;
- opportunities for tutorial support and review of progress.

Staff who need to be involved include:

- specialist APL adviser;
- subject tutors;
- personal tutors;
- internal verifier.

Assessment techniques and methods include:

- compilation of evidence in a portfolio, either individually or with other learners;
- tutorial review of progress;
- assessment and feedback on any gaps, weaknesses etc;
- assessment of practical skills (tests);
- assessment of knowledge and understanding.

Certification

The requirements of learners seeking APL and those putting forward evidence from other learning programmes are the same.

At this stage, learners are seeking:

- confirmation that evidence is suitable for certification;
- formal accreditation;
- a final record of achievement.

Modular programmes mean that APL and certification procedures have to be backed up by good information systems, where individuals progress can be tracked and recorded.

An organization has to provide:

- procedures for recording choices of units, and completion of units;
- regular opportunities for assessment and verification;
- prompt issuing of certificates for individual units.

Staff who need to be involved include:

- APL assessor;
- subject assessor;
- awarding body verifier.

It is clear from this outline of different services and learners' requirements, that systems for accrediting prior learning are an *integral part* of assessment services for all programmes. Assessment and accreditation of prior learning are not, therefore, exclusive or different; they are part of good assessment practice.

Tensions and dilemmas

APL as part of an assessment strategy

The vast amount of publicity given to APL has had positive effects on the ways in which many teachers and institution managers have re-considered the entire process of assessing and accrediting achievement for all learners. It has also been central to implementing a modular curriculum and has encouraged more flexibility in how learning activities are offered on all programmes. Individualized learning packages, for example, can help all learners reflect on their past learning and supplement it with concurrent learning. At the same time, the way in which APL has been set up has often led to its isolation from other assessment processes. It is also complex to implement and, in some programmes, it can promise more than it can deliver.

Some learning outcomes lend themselves more easily to evidence from prior experiential learning than others. For example, many practical skills are often easier to prove than some of the cognitive and reflective skills required on professional and academic programmes. This appears to be particularly true where certain learning outcomes can really only be gained through participating in specific processes, and where the presentation of evidence from prior learning is no easier or quicker than going through a conventional programme. APL can therefore be more difficult and complex to manage in programmes where there are no clear definitions of learning outcomes, or where knowledge, understanding and critical analysis of a specialist subject are an important aspect of competence.

For many adults, it can be difficult to sustain motivation unless APL is a quick route to a qualification or to gaining individual units or modules. APL appears to work best when learners have clear goals, a high level of motivation to collect and present evidence in portfolios, and when they have access to a range of evidence that is relatively easy to present and assess.

Coherence and flexibility

Moves towards modular programmes have raised questions about the effects of modularization and credit-based assessment on the coherence of learning programmes. Some commentators fear that in open-ended modular programmes, learners lose the chance to systematically build up specialist skills, to progress from simple to complex concepts, and to see links between diverse subjects. This can be exacerbated by a more fragmented relationship between learners and teachers in different programme teams. Providing support and points of contact for learners is especially necessary where learners are combining modules from different programmes.

Without careful planning, assessment can become similarly fragmented, with some learning outcomes being over- or under-assessed, or the timing of assessments leading to difficulties in learners' workload. Where a modular programme extends over different levels, such as in a degree programme, defining a coherent range of learning outcomes is important.

Other tensions arise from the fragmenting of programme teams, where the implicit socialization about standards, level, and quality is no longer automatically part of discussion between a small group of teachers and programme managers. Assessing evidence from past learning also means that assessment judgements about learners' achievements have to be easily understood, and communicated across boundaries between institutions and between different parts of the education and training system.

Summary

A modular curriculum offers enormous potential for creating flexible and individualized learning programmes. Assessment and accreditation of prior learning require education and training organizations to see a range of assessment services as important for all learners. An assessment strategy enables an organization to consider these requirements and to design a coherent approach to their implementation. Modular programmes require clear documentation and procedures for assessment, backed up by effective information and recording systems. A modular curriculum also raises questions about coherence in learning and mechanisms for combating possible fragmentation of assessment and support for learners.

PURPOSE OF ASSESSMENT	LEARNER WANTS	ORGANIZATION PROVIDES/HAS ACCESS TO
Initial guidance – to enable learner to make choices based on clear information about options and own abilities	– assessment for career direction – assessment for aptitude – design of a learning agreement or action plan – review and assessment of prior learning – assessment to select appropriate programme Assessment is carried out jointly between learner and person in guidance role	– database of organizational, local and national programmes – details of modules, assessment/accreditation/ progression route – details of other agencies' APL arrangements and provision – information on costs/fees/grants – access to diagnostic work experience placements
Entry to programmes – To provide information for teacher/manager of programme – To provide learner with a programme that meets needs abilities and aspirations	– entry to learning programme without having traditional entry qualifications – decision about suitability for accreditation for parts of the programme via APL – assessment of prior learning Assessment is carried out by person making entry decision	– database of organizational programmes, modules, and entry requirements – details of acceptable entry alternatives, specific credits given to different qualifications – awarding body guidelines for APL – interview guidelines
Programme – To provide information to teachers and learners about progress, achievements and future needs	– assessment of prior learning – review of progress – recognition of achievement – diagnosis of further needs/learning targets – opportunities to record achievements Assessment is carried out jointly between teachers and learners	– learning action plan – tutorial support for review and guidance – access to a bank of flexible and open learning assignments – review of progress and diagnostic assessment
Certification – To provide information for teachers and learners about progress, achievements and future needs	– to be able to articulate what she has gained – proof of attainment in the form of certificate/record of achievement – formal accreditation of prior learning Assessment is carried out by person certificating achievement	– employee/HE application procedures – HE admissions requirements – flexible payment/registration certification arrangements.

STAFF INVOLVED	AGENCIES/PEOPLE WHO OFFER THE SERVICE	TECHNIQUES AND METHODS
– careers officer/advisor – guidance worker – central admissions – vocational/academic staff – TEC staff – assessment and accreditation manager	– guidance services – central admissions – vocational/academic programme areas – higher education admissions and academic staff – Open College Network (OCN) tutors – Adult Education (AE) staff	– personal guidance interview – careers interest guides – learner self-assessment exercises – assessing current competencies – skills – work experience for assessment and diagnosis of aptitude – initial diagnostic assessment – guidance interview; general/subject-specific – portfolio building workshops
– APL advisor – APL guidance/mentor – vocational/academic tutor/trainer – assessment/accreditation manager – HE admissions staff	– college vocational/academic programme – college central admissions/assessment unit – HE admissions – OCN tutors – AE tutors	– assessing skills, knowledge and understanding – examination of references, application letters, portfolios – selection interview: formal and informal – tests

– personal tutor
– vocational/academic subject staff
– counsellor/guidance worker
– workplace assessor/line manager/supervisor
	– organization where learning programme take place:
	  • individual staff
	  • college assessment unit
	– OCN tutors
	– AE tutors
		– learning contract
		– in-course portfolio compilation
		– recording achievement
		– learning assignments
		– one-to-one/group/peer review
		– skills tests
		– a wide range of assessment exercises – oral, written, practical

– personal tutor – vocational/academic assessors – awarding body moderator/verifier – careers officer/ guidance worker	– vocational/academic staff – central assessment unit – OCN tutors – AE tutors	– summative record of achievement – end-of-course portfolio – end-of-course example/test/assignment

Figure 4.3 *Summary of assessment processes (Ecclestone, 1994)*

Further reading

Practical guidelines and background

Challis, M (1993) *Introducing APEL*, Routledge, London.
Ecclestone, K (1994) *Understanding Assessment*, NIACE, Leicester.
Field, M (1993) *APL: Developing more flexible colleges*, Routledge, London.
Further Education Development Agency (1995) *A Framework for Credit: Guidelines 2, learning outcomes, units and modules*, FEDA, London.
Further Education Development Agency (1995) *A Framework for Credit: a common framework for post-14 education and training for the twenty-first century*, FEDA, London.
Nasta, T (1994) *How to Design a Vocational Curriculum*, Kogan Page, London.

Consideration of practical and wider issues
Fraser, W (1995) *Learning from Experience: Empowerment or Incorporation?*, NIACE, Leicester.

5 Diagnosing Learners' Needs

Different forms of diagnostic assessment help learners to be more effective and autonomous in their learning. Although diagnostic assessment underpins formative assessment and therefore has a crucial role in learning, many people associate it with the type of testing carried out by educational psychologists for learners with learning difficulties. Recently, it has been more widely associated with initial diagnostic testing in colleges and schools for literacy and numeracy skills, and particularly with the Basic Skills Agency's diagnostic tests for literacy and numeracy. Diagnostic assessment is also increasingly used as part of a more informal process of guidance which aims to help learners decide on their options before applying to join a particular programme.

Diagnostic assessment fulfils a formative function of diagnosing strengths and weaknesses to help learners and teachers make decisions about what needs to be done next and to improve learning. It also fulfils a summative function as a basis for making a decision about someone's suitability for entry to a programme or module. There is a wide range of tests and assessments for diagnostic assessment, covering formal tests for literacy and numeracy, tests for establishing career direction, as well as more general ways of assessing attributes and abilities.

Changes to funding, and the way in which the vocational curriculum is designed and managed, have affected how institutions see the role of diagnostic assessment. The emphasis given by funding criteria to high retention and completion rates require teachers and managers in schools and colleges to ensure that learners enter the right programmes and stay on them. Diagnostic assessment is seen as an important aspect of this. Growing interest in modular programmes also makes diagnostic assessment a necessary part of helping learners progress through increasingly complex programmes. The range of learners who receive diagnostic assessment, therefore, varies considerably: some institutions screen certain groups while others screen all their full-time learners. Managing diagnostic assessment to meet requirements for funding and curriculum organization requirements, raises strategic and resource issues as well as educational ones.

However, diagnostic assessment is not only about the types of initial assessment described above. It is also a central – and often overlooked – aspect of formative assessment, and it plays a crucial role in raising learners' achievements and motivating them to be effective in *how* they learn, as well as in what they learn. Diagnostic assessment, when used well, enables people to learn about learning. In their everyday interactions with groups and individual learners, teachers use many processes of diagnosis in order to find out the barriers which learners have, and to find ways of helping them become more autonomous learners. These processes might include both formal and informal assessment, but teachers rarely refer to this as 'diagnostic assessment'. To raise an awareness of the wider scope of diagnostic assessment's role in the vocational curriculum, an assessment strategy will need to counter the image of diagnostic assessment as being limited to initial testing of skills and abilities. Otherwise, there is a danger that teachers will not see it as central to good teaching and effective learning.

This chapter focuses on two distinct uses of diagnostic assessment: initial diagnosis and guidance, designed to identify learners' needs at the start of their programme, and the broader role of diagnostic assessment in the learning process itself. It aims to:

- identify different stages where diagnostic assessment can be used;
- examine the role of diagnostic assessment in teaching and learning
- examine how organizations can manage the implications of collecting and handling information about learners.

Initial diagnostic assessment

Diagnostic assessment can provide information for teachers, learners, and for managers of institutions at different stages in a learning programme. Initial diagnostic assessment can be useful in several different ways, including:

- *Initial guidance* can help learners recognize their existing achievements and make informed decisions about which programme to apply for (formative assessment).
- *Initial screening and diagnostic assessment* can identify a learner's requirements for different types of support, such as for literacy and numeracy and study skills (formative assessment).
- *Initial diagnostic assessment* can enable an institution to make a decision about selection for a particular programme, or about whether someone is eligible to seek accreditation of their prior learning (summative assessment).

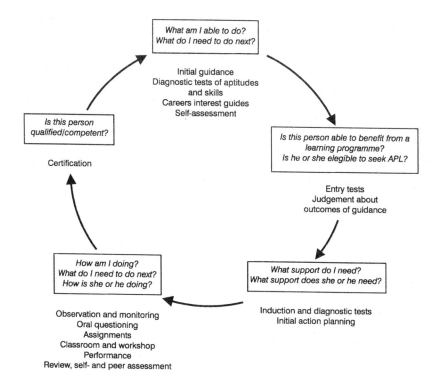

Figure 5.1 *Diagnostic assessment at different stages in a learning programme*

Pre-programme guidance

For many learners, deciding which programme or qualification to undertake can be a confusing and threatening process. For schools, colleges and universities, the aim of offering impartial guidance is often undermined by competition from other organizations, or a perception that learners who are progressing from one stage to another in the same organization do not need initial guidance for the next stage. It can be useful to see initial guidance as an assessment process which offers new learners – and those already in the institution who might be changing direction or starting something new – the chance to assess their previous achievements, and relate them to future goals.

Outcomes and activities
This formative assessment provides:

- *General information* about someone's aspirations, skills, knowledge and aptitude which can confirm their choice about which qualification or programme is most suitable.
- *Specific information* about someone's skills, knowledge and aspirations in relation to a particular programme, in order to establish the appropriate level of study, to identify requirements for different types of support and to show how previous achievements match what will be covered in the programme.
- *The basis for an initial action plan* which shows possible routes for progression, including combinations of modules from different programmes, and the specific support – for example in core skills – which learners might need.

Assessment for these purposes can thus be informal and exploratory, or more formal and focused. It might use a learner's own criteria for making joint decisions about the next step or use more prescriptive, externally set criteria.

Activities might include:

- *counselling* to enable individuals to define and clarify their aspirations;
- *guidance* about options and possibilities;
- *discussions* about evidence of achievement in a portfolio or record of achievement;
- *formal assessment* of skills and attributes.

Using the information

Assessment as part of pre-programme guidance helps learners make better decisions about which programme to apply for. At this stage, it is part of a two-way process between the learner and someone in a guidance role; this might be a teacher, course leader, admissions tutor or careers officer.

Some of the information gained from this assessment can be used at subsequent stages, but it is important to clarify with learners which information is automatically passed on and which is confidential between the learner and the person in a guidance role. For example, the results of diagnostic tests might be passed to other teachers who will be working with the learner, or to staff responsible for providing support in basic skills and core skills. An assessment strategy can enable an organization to consider how to manage diagnostic assessment and to decide:

- which groups of learners need diagnostic assessment at the initial guidance stage, and for what purpose;
- what will be assessed and which methods will be used;
- who the information will be passed to;

- which information systems provide the least bureaucratic, yet most efficient way of recording and communicating information.

Selection

Initial diagnostic assessment can also be used to enable admissions tutors and programme leaders to make decisions about entry to a programme. *Assessment activities might include:*

- *entry tests* – for example, to assess literacy and numeracy, academic ability or practical skills;
- *selection interview* and a recommendation for entry to a programme;
- *a decision* that a candidate is able to seek accreditation of prior learning for individual modules, or for a whole programme, where this is appropriate.

Organizational requirements

Education and training organizations improve initial guidance and diagnostic assessment if they adopt a strategic approach to implementing processes for it to take place, and if teachers and learners are aware of its different purposes. A strategy can coordinate processes for providing diagnostic assessment across different programme and curriculum areas. This helps to avoid piecemeal approaches or duplication of resources, and enables good practice to be shared.

Diagnostic assessment produces information about learners which can be the basis of feedback to them and to other teachers where this is appropriate. An organization needs to identify what should be done with this information, and to implement procedures for meeting needs for follow-up support.

Growing numbers of schools, colleges and universities are developing:

- charts of their provisions which show the range of modules and combinations which are available, with entry requirements for each one (modules might be completely open access, or require some previous experience, or require another module to be taken in conjunction with it);
- maps of progression routes into, across and beyond the organizations;
- information about procedures for the accreditation of prior learning and any restrictions on this, such as core modules which need to be undertaken in a learning programme;
- a range of initial assessment activities for different skills and attributes;
- procedures for passing on information where this is appropriate for identifying and providing support in specific skills;
- an organization-wide system for learning support, coordinated by one person.

Diagnostic assessment in learning programmes

Colleges, schools and universities are increasingly being funded for their ability to retain learners on the various programmes for which they have enrolled, and to make sure they are successful in completing them. This can produce tension between the desire to widen access and the danger of recruiting learners to programmes where they might fail. There is growing interest in diagnostic assessment which can give organizations and learners a better idea of the support that individual learners are likely to need, and how their previous achievements match the intended learning outcomes of a programme. More attention is also being paid to the outcomes of research into measurements of 'value-added' – the 'comparison between the characteristics of learners at entry... and their achievements at exit' (FEDA, 1995b).

Initial screening and diagnostic assessment, and the systematic collection of data, have become more important. They help learners to make informed decisions about which programme to join, and enable teachers and managers of institutions to provide the right kinds of support during the programme which will enhance learners' chances of success.

Diagnostic assessment is also an ongoing process. For many teachers, the process of working out the difficulties which groups or individual learners might have in the processes and activities of learning, is part and parcel of everyday interactions, classroom questions and assessment of course work. It is possible for teachers and learners to make these often intuitive activities more conscious and, as a result, more effective. There is a strong argument for teachers to see diagnostic assessment as being crucial to formative assessment, and therefore as an integral part of learning. If they do this, they can develop skills in 'diagnostic observation' and the types of questions they ask learners, and integrate these with their everyday teaching and assessment.

There are two aspects to this: one is the *formal* process of diagnostic assessment, usually through specific tests or assignments, and the other is an ongoing, more *informal* process which teachers carry out as an everyday part of planning and assessing different activities.

Initial screening and diagnostic assessment

Initial diagnostic assessment in a learning programme can enable teachers and learners to identify what support is needed for developing certain attributes and skills. This can take place at the beginning of a programme – for example, during induction – or at periodic intervals during the programme, according to individual needs.

Assessment activities

This formative assessment provides:

- *specific exercises* to assess direction or aptitude: the Basic Skills Agency tests are often used to assess literacy and numeracy needs, but there is a wide range of tests which assess aptitude and vocational interests, learning styles, practical abilities, learning difficulties or disabilities;
- *specific exercises* to establish previous achievements in core skills and any particular needs for support in developing them;
- *a basis for measuring abilities at the beginning* of a programme, which can be statistically compared learners' level of achievement on exit;

A number of schools and colleges have been involved in research for systematically predicting learners' A-level grades based on data about their GCSE attainments. The A-level information system (ALIS) has shown a strong correlation between GCSE and A-level scores, and some organizations are using this to analyse other patterns, such as differences between different subject achievements, or the effects of providing learning support to strong, weak and middle ability learners. FEDA is currently piloting other ways of measuring 'value added' for learners in GNVQ programmes. (FEDA, 1995b).

Diagnostic assessment and the collection of data for monitoring activities, and for providing different types of learning support, can take place during an induction period, or at the beginning of different stages in a learning programme.

Using the information

The same issues about how information should be communicated to other staff which were outlined for initial guidance, affect how diagnostic assessment is carried out at the beginning of a learning programme and at various points during it. Assessment of core and basic skills produces information about further support which needs to be communicated to other staff in the organization, as well as to learners. An assessment strategy can consider methods of recording this information based on evaluation of effective practice from different programme teams.

A vital part of learning

Once learners have embarked on a learning programme, teachers can use diagnostic assessment in teaching and learning activities, and use the outcomes to modify activities or set different targets for them.

Outcomes and activities
This formative assessment provides:

- diagnosis of how an individual engages with the learning process, to find out barriers and difficulties, learning styles and approaches;
- information for learners about how they learn and the strategies they use effectively or ineffectively.

The assessment activities to achieve these outcomes might be formal and planned in advance, such as course work or other assessments designed for a particular formative purpose, or arise informally from tutorials, and observations of learners in classroom and workshop activities.

Focusing on potential achievements
Diagnostic assessment in a learning programme focuses on a person's learning *potential*. This potential is, Gipps (1995) argues, not something which is fixed but dynamic. It therefore responds to the support teachers can give to learners in helping them to reach it. If teachers consciously set out to assess how learners respond to tasks and questions, they can use the information from this assessment in their planning. It can thus enable them to make decisions about what to include in assignments or learning activities based on how ready learners are to do something, and what extra support they need. They can also help learners become more independent, not by merely 'leaving them to get on with the work', but by deliberately fostering the skills to assess their own performance and to recognize success and high quality work.

These skills are the basis for criteria used to allocate grades of distinction and merit in GNVQs, since these are based on learners' autonomy and independence in carrying out tasks. They are also an important aspect of the skills and qualities sought in degree level work: progress towards higher degree classifications is partly based on autonomy and independence, on learners being able to assess and monitor their own achievement, and to set new targets.

Formal and informal diagnosis
In the context of everyday learning, diagnostic assessment is a powerful and often overlooked subset of formative assessment. Teachers' informal or formal diagnosis is only formative when it is used actively and consciously to close the gap between someone's performance and the standard they are aiming for. There are two main types of diagnostic assessment in a learning programme:

- assessment which is an informal part of teachers' observation and monitoring of everyday classroom and tutorial assessments;

- more formal, specifically designed assessments which might help a learner recognize his or her strengths and weaknesses, and where the teacher provides more systematic and considered feedback.

If formative assessment is differentiated in this way, teachers and learners clarify which assessments are used to diagnose learning, where feedback is provided to help learners do better next time, and those assessments which teachers might call 'formative', but which are more precisely part of recording achievements for summative assessment and/or grading purposes, and which constitute *continuous summative* assessment.

Learning how to learn

When it is used well, assessment provides learners with a powerful impetus to monitor and evaluate their own learning. Diagnostic and formative assessment are not only concerned with what learners know or can do, but more importantly to try to discover *how* they know something (or do not), how they are (or are not) able to demonstrate different skills, and what the *barriers* are to achievement. These barriers might be linked to the learning or assessment task itself, the way the programme is organized, or to personal or private issues affecting the learner. In using formative assessment to shed light on how people learn, teachers can link this to considering their learners' individual styles and approaches to learning. Gipps (1995) points out that for this to be effective, learners need:

- a proper understanding of the standard being aimed for (the criteria), which they have internalized for themselves;
- a grasp of what constitutes a 'high quality' piece of work;
- the chance to compare their actual level of performance with the teacher's perception of the standard;
- an understanding of what action must be taken to close the gap which they have internalized for themselves.

It is clear that this entails more than just ensuring that learners are covering all the requirements laid down by the awarding body: it means that teachers and learners have to see assessment as integral to the processes of learning rather than a set of procedures to get through.

Communicating the criteria

'I can tell at a glance whether it's a distinction or a merit' (College lecturer)
'When it comes to grading the work 'merit' or 'distinction', I ask the students to 'bid' for their grade and to convince me why they should have it' (GNVQ school teacher)

For many experienced teachers, the standards that learners are aiming for are tacit. Teachers accumulate a wealth of this tacit knowledge over time, and it is often buried deep in their individual subconcious, and implicitly shared with other teachers in the same subject or programme area who have also internalized what the standards mean. However, translating this knowledge so that learners can internalize it for themselves is difficult. Research into the feedback which teachers commonly give to learners (Winter, 1994 and Gipps, 1995) seems to show that teachers find it hard to articulate their notions about standards and the required level of work.

This tacit sense of the standards also explains why changes to an assessment system – such as the move from A-levels to GNVQs or from BTEC programmes to GNVQs – can initially be very disorientating and demotivating for experienced teachers. It throws them back to all the uncertainties of being a novice teacher who, like all novices, has to learn what the new standards are. However, when teachers have the chance to discuss standards and criteria with other teachers and with external verifiers, their sense of what constitutes excellence or poor performance is greatly enhanced. If learners are involved in a similar process of moderation, and discussion about standards, they are more likely to internalize the standard as well. Peer and self-assessment can be powerful aids to this, and therefore a crucial part of formative assessment.

There are a number of barriers to communicating the criteria, including:

- Teachers may not realize the importance of this and may not be trained how to help learners understand the criteria.
- Feedback may not enable learners to identify the necessary standard and/or how to work out the next steps for improving their performance.
- Pressure on time and the external demands for summative assessment can hinder formative assessment unless it is explicitly planned for.
- Grading and the pressure to gain individual competencies or pass external tests can get in the way of taking notice of feedback because learners (and teachers) become distracted by the impact of the grade or the number of competencies still left to attain.
- Frequent changes to the composition of programme teams can hinder the chance to develop a shared sense of standards and quality, and to feel confident in moderating each others' assessment judgements.

Giving effective feedback
'You have covered the necessary content. However, you have completely failed to present your work coherently or logically. You need to pay much more attention to this next time' (College lecturer's written feedback)
'A stunningly original, analytical and thorough piece of work' (College lecturer's written feedback)

Teachers often carry out a great deal of diagnostic assessment, and record information and observations about learners from it. Much of this is carried in their heads, some of it is written down. They might pass on this information to other teachers, such as the outcomes of tests for literacy and numeracy. But this information does not become *feedback* unless it is then used to make a difference to learners' performance, and communicated in ways that learners can understand for themselves.

As the above quotes show, many teachers spend a good deal of time giving informal and formal feedback to learners about how well they are, or are not, doing. This takes different forms, including:

- *annotating learners' work* through marking assignments;
- *discussing progress* in tutorials;
- *giving oral or written feedback* about strengths and weaknesses;
- *responding to immediate observations* in classrooms and workshops and to learners' verbal and non-verbal responses.

Although teachers often comment on different strengths and weaknesses, it seems that much of this assessment feedback may not actually enable learners to grasp the standard, or recognize what action is needed to reach it. Good feedback is a complex skill, but if assessment is to be truly diagnostic and formative, learners have to internalize what is being aimed for and what constitutes excellent and poor work. Teachers' feedback needs to enable learners to learn how to monitor and regulate their own work so that they can work out for themselves how to achieve the standard. Once they can do this, they have to compare what they actually do with the teacher's expectations.

Developing and using exemplars

'Assessment should display to the learner models of performance that can be evaluated and also, indicate the assistance, experiences and forms of practice required by learners as they move towards more competent performance' (Glaser, 1990 cited by Gipps, 1995)

'I collect the best and worst bits from the students' assignments and put them together as examples of a typical assignment. Then I ask the students to imagine they are the teacher and to mark the 'assignment' using my mark sheet and the criteria. I do this after they've had their own work back' (Certificate in Education tutor)

In GNVQs, teachers across a wide range of vocational areas are provided with exemplars of good and poor work, with extensive notes about how to interpret the criteria for them. These can be a useful aid, especially if they generate discussion about quality and standards, because this makes it easier for teachers to articulate these ideas to learners.

Teachers and learners can also generate their own exemplars. Teachers might, for example, take actual examples – anonymous of course! – from learners' work and compile them into an exemplar. After learners have had their own work returned with feedback, they can work in groups to mark the exemplar using the teachers' mark scheme and criteria. This process teaches them about the process of assessment and enables them to identify what is needed in the exemplar to gain a better mark. Some school and college programme teams have begun to create a programme portfolio of exemplars based on learners' work, which provides a basis for discussion about standards and quality.

Using peer and self-assessment

'I don't like letting students assess themselves or each other. It just becomes an argument; your assessment versus their assessment!' (GNVQ teacher)

'For a *distinction* you must show that, in looking back at the work you have done, you have given a detailed explanation of why you approached the work in the way you did. You must also show that you have thought about alternative ways of tackling the work and how this might have helped you achieve your targets... You must also show that you have considered ways in which you would improve the work if you were to repeat it' (NCVQ, 1995)

Once learners become more confident and knowledgeable about assessing the required standard, carefully planned *peer and self-assessment* can help them to assess each other and give feedback. For certain skills such as team work and problem solving, self-and peer assessment are often more valid than the teachers'. Yet in spite of the powerful effect that peer and self-assessment can have on helping learners understand the criteria and in monitoring their own learning, some teachers feel uncomfortable when learners have different judgements from their own. It helps to be very clear about whether the peer assessment is formative or summative, and to enable learners to make more effective use of it by teaching them about assessment processes and purposes. The grading criteria used in GNVQs can provide valuable opportunities to review and assess how a particular piece of work was carried out, monitored and evaluated.

Collaborating to reach the goal

'I feel guilty when I see the students making unnecessary mistakes, but the criteria for GNVQs mean that they have to work on their own... so I can't help them' (GNVQ college lecturer)

Just as the purpose of summative assessment has tended to distort our perceptions about what assessment is for, the legacy of testing, examinations and grades also affects many people's views about how assessment should be carried out. Images of assessment often conjure up learners having to memorize facts and knowledge, having only one chance in a one-off performance, doing the assessment task unaided in an unfamiliar or artificial environment.

This image of assessment is obviously less accurate in GNVQs and NVQs, but there can still be uncertainty about the conditions for setting up assessment, especially where criteria emphasize autonomy in planning or carrying out tasks. As a result, many teachers feel uncomfortable with the degree to which they should or should not be helping learners with an assessment task. Clarifying whether the assessment is summative or formative is useful in deciding whether it requires collaboration between teachers and learners – in diagnostic and formative assessment, it is necessary for enhancing learning before a summative assessment.

A more carefully constructed approach to assessment in the learning process may help to clarify the potential role of teachers and learners. The work of the educational psychologist Vygotsky is attracting growing interest in relation to formative and diagnostic assessment (see Gipps, 1995). Research is being carried out into how teachers collaborate with learners in order to make the most of formative and diagnostic assessment in the National Curriculum. Work currently being undertaken by researchers at the Institute of Education has relevant lessons for teachers in schools, colleges and universities, and further research in this area would tell us more about how teachers of adults and young people use diagnostic assessment. Two areas from school-based research might be of interest. These are:

- Teachers can observe the gap between the *actual* level of a learner's unassisted performance, and his or her *potential* level in a performance when she or he is supported by a teacher's guidance or in collaboration with more capable peers (the zone of *proximal development*).
- Teachers can consciously design and implement a process of planned support and guidance to help people perform at a higher level, with the support being gradually removed as a person becomes more competent (*Scaffolding*).

Both these processes provide diagnostic information for teachers, so that they can design challenging but realistic tasks, and assist learners to gain 'mastery'. There is, then, considerable overlap between the way that learners and teachers collaborate in teaching and learning activities, and collaborative assessment. If teachers see part of their role in formative and diagnostic assessment as *collaborative*, they can avoid the 'hit and miss' approach of letting learners work on their own too soon, or learning too much through 'trial and error'. Both can be demotivating and lead to failure.

Recording achievement
  'There's so much paper work and so much recording to do that there's no time
  for learning' (GNVQ school teacher)
  'When I look back over what I've done, I realize that I've become a lot better at
  thinking about what I do. I write down what's gone well and I use the written
  feedback from my tutor to see if I've covered all the points she raised last time I
  did an assignment' (BA student)

Some of the outcomes from on-going diagnostic assessment provide learners with insights into their own learning. Grading criteria for GNVQs, for
example, require learners to monitor, review and evaluate their work, as does
the core skills unit 'Improving own learning and performance'. Evidence
from self-assessment and reviews can be important indications of learners'
progress in these areas during a programme, and for summarizing this at the
end.

However, without careful organization and planning, the formative and
summative purposes of recording achievements and reflecting on them can
become onerous for learners and teachers.

INFORMAL	FORMAL
• monitoring and observing individuals and groups	• marking assignments and projects and relating feedback to information from informal observation
• watching out for verbal and non-verbal signs of confusion about an assessment task	• making notes for particular individuals and verbal feedback to the group
• identifying the barriers to do with the task itself, the way learners approach it, other factors	• explaining to learners how the criteria were interpreted, especially in the poorer work
• giving impromptu feedback	• generating and using exemplars of good and poor performance and requiring learners to mark them
• carrying out informal self- and peer assessment	• carrrying out formal self- and peer assessment

Figure 5.2 *Diagnostic assessment and formative feedback*

Effective diagnostic assessment
For diagnostic assessment to be effective, teachers have to:

● present the standard or goal the learner is aiming for, in ways which she
  or he can understand;

- help learners compare their actual performance with what is required, so that they recognize what action they need to take to close the gap;
- consider carefully the type and scope of feedback they give to learners, so that different learning outcomes are covered at various stages over a period of time, rather than over-assessing some outcomes at the expense of others;
- separate giving grades or results to learners from the process of giving formative feedback;
- acquire good observation and questioning skills in response to different barriers which groups or individuals seem to have;
- clarify the different purposes of assessment with learners so that they can recognize summative, formative and diagnostic functions and take a more active role in them.

Learners have to:

- see the relevance of an assessment task and how it meets particular processes and applications;
- make connections between what they are doing with what they already know and can do;
- work out what they need to be able to carry out a task, and whether they have done enough to meet the criteria;
- question themselves about what they have to do and how well they are doing it.

These tasks and activities for teachers and learners comprise a process which helps learners not just to acquire the skills and knowledge to gain the qualification, but how to learn and assess these for themselves. It is a process of enabling learners to be their own best teacher and assessor!

Barriers to diagnostic assessment

Discussing the criteria

It is apparent, then, that effective feedback to learners should be linked closely to clear standards for achievement and a shared understanding between learners and teachers about how assessment will be carried out. In early GNVQ developments, a criticism levelled by teachers was that too much time was spent working with students to clarify grading criteria and levels of achievement. This may be a feature of the complex jargon of early GNVQ specifications, which may become simpler in light of criticisms made by various government bodies when reviewing GNVQ assessments.

However, instead of being a 'flaw' in the assessment regime, the process of arriving at a *shared* understanding is essential to the effectiveness of diagnostic and formative assessment. It is one of the means by which learners internalize and thoroughly understand what is being asked of them.

Communicating the criteria, therefore, requires a different approach to using time and resources based on the broader view of diagnostic and formative assessment outlined in this chapter. Much of the guidance from awarding bodies, inspectors and curriculum bodies tends to suggest that the process of using formative assessment to enable diagnosis of learning barriers is unproblematic and widely understood. It also tends to underestimate how far the process of having to meet the requirements of summative assessment can distort the role of formative and diagnostic assessment. Discussion with learners needs to supplement the detailed guidance and instructions given to teachers by awarding bodies and the NCVQ. Guidance written specifically for learners by the NCVQ (1995) and exemplars developed by programme teams and the NCVQ (1994a, b, c) can be a good basis for these discussions.

Accumulating evidence

Pressures of time and a detailed assessment system can militate against good formative and diagnostic assessment. There is evidence from GNVQs and NVQs that the onerous requirements for 'amassing evidence' to cover performance criteria and range statements have had undesirable effects on diagnostic assessment. If a learner's performance is 'good enough', it is likely to be signed off against an element of competence. Feedback to learners often focuses on the need to fill gaps in evidence towards summative assessment, rather than fostering active learning or meaningful self-assessment. This can lead to the setting up of artificial learning situations which may add little to learners' understanding. Reductions in the amount of assessment evidence which is required will not automatically result in better feedback or alleviate the tendency to identify 'gaps' in what learners need to cover for summative assessment. For this to happen, an understanding of diagnostic assessment and a strategic approach to its use are both needed.

Summary

Diagnostic assessment can help organizations become more effective in helping learners meet the requirements of a learning programme, and to make informed choices about which programme is most appropriate. It can provide a systematic basis for collecting information about learners' needs for support, which can be passed on to staff responsible for co-ordinating this support, or to other tutors and teachers. However, it can also generate a great deal of information which can, if not carefully managed, become too onerous for teachers and learners to use effectively. If information is collated and monitored as part of an organization's quality assurance, it can also provide valuable and fascinating data for evaluating achievements and the effects of different factors at entry and during a programme.

Diagnosis is also a central feature of good teaching and effective formative feedback. It enables teachers and learners to consider consciously and strategically how to achieve the goal of self-monitoring learners who can reflect on their learning, build on existing skills and set their own targets. This goal, however, is hindered by poor feedback, implicit or hidden criteria and a limited range of assessment methods. It is enhanced by good qualitative oral and written feedback and discussion between teachers and with learners about standards and exemplars of performance.

An assessment strategy can help organizations consider the implications of diagnostic assessment and plan how to make best use of the information in generates.

Further reading

Practical information and guidelines
Further Education Development Agency (1995) *Learning Styles*, FEDA, London.
Further Education Development Agency (1995b) *Current developments in value added*, FEDA, London.
Further Education Development Agency (1994) *Implementing GNVQs – a manual*, FEDA, London.
National Council for Vocational Qualifications (1995) *Grading Advanced Business GNVQ*, NCVQ, London.
National Council for Vocational Qualifications (1994a) *Assessing students' work in Manufacturing*, NCVQ, London.
National Council for Vocational Qualifications (1994b) *Assessing students' work in Leisure and Tourism*, NCVQ, London.
National Council for Vocational Qualifications (1994c) *Assessing students' work in Art and Design*, NCVQ, London.

Background issues
Gipps, C (1995) *Beyond testing: towards a theory of educational assessment*, Falmer Press, London.
Rowntree, D (1986) *Assessing Students: how shall we know them?*, Kogan Page, London
Torrance, H (ed) (1995) *Evaluating Authentic Assessment*, Open University Press, Buckingham.
Winter, R (1994) 'Levels in the Credit Framework II', *Journal for Further and Higher Education*, Spring 1994, Vol 17.

6 Records of Achievement and Portfolios

Records of achievement (RoAs) have grown in importance in assessment systems at all levels of the education and training system, as part of an attempt to provide a better, more extensive account of learners' achievements. Development of RoAs in schools and colleges throughout the 1980s were given an important government impetus in 1984, with a policy statement by the then Department of Education and Science accompanied by funding for local initiatives to develop RoAs. Further interest was generated by funding for the Technical and Vocational Education Initiative and the Certificate in Pre-Vocational Education, which fostered a great deal of staff and curriculum development activity. This interest reflected a wider concern that assessment could potentially play a much more educational and motivational role than it had in the past. Records of achievement were also seen to provide employers, and other education and training organizations with a better and more accurate account of what learners could actually do, than the traditional reporting of single grades and lists of examination results. They can report on abilities and aptitudes which have been assessed but which are not traditionally reported. The latest manifestation of this movement – the National Record of Achievement for all school leavers – includes the results of summative assessments in the form of examination results, as well as other accounts of achievement.

Teachers' interest in the development of portfolios and RoAs, for both younger and adult learners, has been fuelled by a commitment to certain principles about learning. These emphasize the use of people's broader life and work experiences as a source of learning, and the motivating role of RoAs in enabling learners to diagnose their own learning and reflect on its implications for what they want to do next. An RoA can therefore be part of a formative and diagnostic process, where learners record achievements and plan further learning. This leads to a summative account of what has been achieved, which can then be used by employers and further and higher education admissions tutors to predict future success.

Recently, the advent of NVQs and GNVQs has introduced a new

dimension to records of achievement, with the use of portfolios of evidence to show the attainment of competencies. Learners accumulate evidence of achievement in portfolios, and then submit a final version for assessment and verification of achievement. Although GNVQs promote a strong formative and motivating function for this process, portfolios also have a powerful summative role in the vocational curriculum, with an emphasis on meeting external specifications of what should be recorded and reported on. They have been particularly popular in programmes where learners seek assessment and accreditation of prior learning. RoAs and portfolios illustrate some tensions and dilemmas in assessment, and their history shows that managing and implementing them is a complex process.

This chapter aims to:

- differentiate between RoAs, profiles and portfolios;
- show the formative and summative roles of RoAs in the vocational curriculum;
- outline some of the issues which RoAs raise for teachers and managers.

Terminology

Records of achievement

Most school-leavers now progress into college, universities or employment training schemes with a National Record of Achievement. This contains a list of their examination results and a testimonial of achievement produced by the school. When these were introduced in the late 1980s, the intention was that this record should be used in three ways:

- as the basis of initial guidance;
- for making decisions about entry to learning programmes or training schemes;
- as a continuing record to be updated through further training at work and in formal education.

RoAs have evolved from their early developments, when they were locally designed and implemented, into a standardized national document which forms part of summative assessment.

Profiles

Debates in the 1980s about what a record of achievement should contain, and how it should be used, drew an important distinction between *profiles* and *records*. Some saw a profile as an extensive total picture of someone, which described strengths and weaknesses and included the type of curriculum vitae which now forms the National Record. This detailed summative profile was arrived at through a continuous assessment process, which documented learners' abilities and provided a basis for review and action planning. Some profiles, such as those developed by the City and Guilds in pre-vocational programmes, had statements about a particular skill – numeracy or communicating with others, for example – on a grid or scale. Other profiles are much more open-ended, and are sometimes based on the criteria which learners set and negotiated themselves.

Depending on the design of the profile, teachers and learners jointly agree progression in different skills and attributes using a numerical rating scale, or by selecting an appropriate statement from a pre-defined bank, or by simply discussing these in more general ways. These profiles aim to build up a broad picture of achievement, covering practical and technical skills, personal qualities, interpersonal skills, numeracy and other areas. The intention in early developments of profiles was that they could be summarized for a final record of achievement.

The progress profile developed by City and Guilds for a vocational preparation course in the 1980s, consisted of banks of statements (a profile 'grid') in communication, practical and numerical skills, social skills and decision-making. The statements are arranged in a hierarchy, with autonomy and initiative as criteria for defining statements in the different levels. This profile aimed to develop a system which would record students' progress within the curriculum, promote their maturity and self confidence, and provide a reliable profile report (Stratton in Broadfoot, 1986). The example below is taken from this profile:

Working in a group
Can cooperate with others when asked
Can work with other members of the group to achieve common aims
Can understand own position and results of own actions within a group
Can be an active and decisive member of a group
Can adopt a variety of roles in a group
(CGLI, 1986, cited by Stratton)

Stratton notes that in 1986, the formats of formative profiles and summative records of achievement were moving further apart. The grid profiles developed in the '80s provided a chart for plotting progress, which was intended to be motivating for learners. The graded statements enabled the 'best' performance to be picked out and summarized for the final record of achievement.

Portfolios

For many people, the image of a portfolio is most commonly represented by large leather cases used by art students going for interviews. One dictionary defines it as a 'flat leather case containing loose documents' (Collins Concise Dictionary). In GNVQs and NVQs, a portfolio consists of documentary and practical information and evidence of achievements from someone's past and present experiences. If a learner is using a portfolio to collect evidence towards accreditation, the evidence is usually translated into the specific requirements to show achievement of learning outcomes or competencies, ie it is compiled and presented for an external audience. Other uses of portfolios, such as in programmes like 'Making Your Experience Count', and in certain adult and community education programmes, enable learners to compile as an exploratory, personal record based entirely on their own criteria as a starting point for making decisions about a career or educational change.

A portfolio's primary purpose, and its intended audience determine, its contents and format. In many programmes, a portfolio is a detailed ongoing record of achievement compiled during a course. In the formative stages of accumulating evidence of achievement, the two terms are interchangeable. For the purposes of this chapter, the formative process of recording achievement in GNVQs and NVQs is denoted by the term 'portfolio'.

At the point when a learner presents evidence for summative assessment, a portfolio is edited for the assessor and verifier. It can then be edited further to form the basis for a testimonial or reference in a final record of achievement. However, although the transition from portfolio to record of achievement is often presented as a smooth transition, the logistics of deciding which evidence to present for summative assessment and then for the final record is not a straightforward one, especially where there is a great deal of evidence accumulated over a programme. A final record for NVQs and GNVQs will formally contain a list of units achieved, with an overall grade for GNVQs.

Recording

This involves two processes. One is a reflective and formative recording of relevant or meaningful experiences, which help learners make sense of their learning and evaluate its effectiveness or otherwise. This more reflective or open-ended process can be edited later for summative purposes, but it is an important aspect of the diagnostic processes outlined in Chapter 5. The other recording process is a summative one, and involves selecting and retaining useful, valid and relevant information to go in the record or portfolio. Teachers will also have their own records of learners' progress in order to plan learning activities and evaluate the quality of a learning programme. This information enables teachers to monitor and review learners' progress over a period of time.

For learners compiling a portfolio, more relevant information or better evidence can replace some of the contents as a programme progresses. When a portfolio is edited for summative purposes, it only contains the most useful evidence rather than everything a learner has done.

Reporting

Effective reporting enables teachers and institutions to provide clear and appropriate information to a range of interested parties, such as other teachers, admissions tutors, employers, parents, inspectors or governors. Reporting achievements enables an institution to gain a richer picture of what its learners gain from different programmes. This promotes qualitative ways to measure the 'value added' which learners gain through a particular programme.

Purposes of RoAs and portfolios

Early development of profiles and records of achievement encouraged teachers and learners to focus attention on assessment of a wider range of attributes, skills and qualities than could be encapsulated by examination results. Assessment was seen as central to the *processes* of learning, which led to a fairer and more extensive 'end product' in the form of a useful record of achievement. Notions about what counted as achievement extended to a wide range of school and college activities, and life and work experience. Self-assessment and recording these achievements were therefore important if learners were to be involved actively in assessment. RoAs were seen as much more than a new method of assessment, since the processes of compiling them required teachers and learners to work collaboratively and to see assessment as central to effective learning.

However, records of achievement were also seen as crucial in changing teachers' and institution managers' ideas about how the curriculum should be designed and delivered. TVEI and CPVE, with extensive government and local authority support, initiated a great deal of staff and curriculum development, often through partnerships between schools and colleges. RoAs were mechanisms for bringing together disparate components in a programme, and for putting the idea of 'student-centred learning' at the heart of the curriculum. At the same time, TVEI promoted notions of cross curricular themes such as technology or enterprise which aimed to link different subjects together with vocationally related themes. In TVEI and

CPVE, core skills such as communication and personal development provided a focus for recording achievement. These different uses for assessing and recording achievement enabled evidence of achievement to be generated from pastoral and tutorial activities, education/industry links, work and community experience and programmes of personal and social development

Where learners combine elements of both vocational and academic programmes, RoAs have an important function in linking common themes and skills across different modules or units. In some schools and colleges, learners can combine parts of GCSEs with GNVQs, or parts of A-levels with GNVQs, or units of competence in NVQs with GNVQs. This is still relatively rare, but as modular programmes become more popular, such combinations will become more common and an RoA can play a central part in bringing coherence to them.

Formative assessment

Records of achievement and portfolios can have a powerful role in formative assessment, by increasing learners' involvement in assessment processes, enabling them to see their strengths and weaknesses and setting targets for future learning.

RoAs and portfolios for formative purposes emphasize self-assessment and a more exploratory, learner-centred and open-ended approach to what might be included. In some areas of adult education, and in early uses of RoAs in schools and colleges, the design, format and content were – and still sometimes are – entirely determined by the learners themselves.

Portfolios as part of the learning process
Portfolios are used in:

- *professional development programmes,* such as teacher and nurse training and often take the form of 'reflective' journals, sometimes with records of incidents and the learning they generated;
- *programmes for adults who might be returning to formal education,* and who need to establish what they have learned over a period of time and where it might lead them to next;
- *GNVQs and NVQs* to show evidence of competence against specific assessment criteria.

Professional development programmes
Many professional programmes foster skills of being able to reflect on experience, and turn this reflection into learning, as essential attributes of being a *professional.* The process of compiling a portfolio or record of this reflection is seen as part of the learning process, where it is used as a vehicle

for translating experiences into a set of outcomes which reflects the learning which has taken place. It might also be summatively assessed as evidence of someone's ability to reflect effectively on their professional practice.

'Making your experience count'

The same sort of process is also used in programmes which aim to help learners who may be returning to education after a break, so that they can assess what they have learned from life and work experiences. Portfolios can be exploratory, reflective and personal, based on someone's personal targets for learning and with an emphasis on self-assessment and reflection. Programmes which provide opportunities for portfolios as part of the learning process encourage learners to see their life and work experience as a rich source of learning, to be able to reflect on particular experiences and make the learning outcomes of this reflection explicit. In doing this, learners might undertake a completely open-ended self-assessment of their life experiences and skills, or they might use specific checklists or profiles. Compiling a portfolio requires them to set out their experiences and the learning outcomes they produced in a logical and structured way. This structure is important if they are going to go on to the process of translating this evidence of learning into a format which can be put forward for accreditation. (For more details about Accreditation of Prior Experiential Learning see Chapter 8.)

GNVQs and NVQs

Portfolios in GNVQs are intended to play a formative and self-assessment role. GNVQs require learners to set targets for learning and assessment in an action plan, and identify opportunities to gain evidence against assessment criteria. Portfolios are records of assignments and other projects, and a means of identifying gaps in evidence. The processes of learners assessing their own work, showing independence in planning and carrying out different activities, are especially important since they form the basis for a final distinction or merit grade. These skills are also involved in the core skills unit 'Improving own performance'. Action planning, self-assessment, reviewing and evaluating the quality of both the final product and the processes that led to it, are designed in GNVQs to be built into a systematic approach to recording achievements and assembling evidence in a portfolio.

In NVQs, portfolios have tended to have a continuous summative function, where learners compile very specific evidence to claim achievement of individual elements and then units of competence. The criteria in the elements and units of competence therefore constrain how the evidence must be presented. The process of submitting this and discussing it with an assessor may lead to the formative role envisaged in GNVQs, but it has not been an explicit intention of the assessment process.

In different vocational programmes, the portfolio which someone produces will be used in different ways, including:

- *to build confidence and self-awareness* and the skills of reflection and self-assessment
- *as evidence of achievement* for applying for a job or formal learning programme;
- *as a basis for claiming accreditation* of a unit or whole qualification.

Summative assessment

RoAs provide a detailed account of activities, achievements, qualities and learning experiences as a report for employers and other education and training organizations, which can be updated as learners progress through education and training programmes.

Portfolios for accreditation
A portfolio of evidence presented for summative purposes is structured by learners' knowledge of what is required for employment or for a particular qualification. In GNVQs and NVQs, the formative and exploratory function of a portfolio is heavily steered by the specifications of criteria which learners must meet. It is clear that there is a fine line between a portfolio which is incorporated into a learning programme as part of the learning process, and one which might provide evidence of achievement for accreditation. However, portfolios which are intended as the basis for accreditation will usually have different features from those used formatively, since they will have been edited and presented specifically for this purpose.

The competencies, skills and knowledge which make up the basis for accreditation determine the content and format of the final portfolio, which consists of extensive evidence of achievement, cross-referenced and edited to match the specifications in the qualification. There are two categories of evidence which make up a summative portfolio. These are:

- *Direct evidence* is directly attributable to the learner and is usually a product of his or her own work. It can include samples of things which the learner has made, produced or created, and videos of activities or processes they have taken part in. This direct evidence might come from previous work and life experiences, or be generated specifically to meet a particular competence for the purposes of the portfolio. Results of tests, written assignments and other assessment activities can therefore be included. In addition to evidence generated from actual past or present performance, assessors can ask questions to support or extend evidence in the portfolio.

- *Indirect evidence* is generated from external sources about the learner. It can include employer's letters, testimonials, references, certificates of training courses and other comments on the learner's work or achievements. Like direct evidence, these might be from the past or from current activities and experiences.

Recent interest in accreditation of prior learning has placed the emphasis heavily on evidence of achievement from past experiences. In reality, many portfolios which are put forward for APL, usually consist of evidence that is generated relatively easily from past achievements, and evidence from concurrent learning assessed in more conventional ways, such as a simulated activity, test or written assignment.

Compiling and assessing a portfolio

A portfolio consists of recorded and documented achievements and reflections on concurrent learning. If it is being used for accreditation in NVQs and GNVQs, the extensive requirements for assessment in these programmes can generate vast amounts of evidence (and confusion) in how to present it. Cross-referencing, editing and imaginative paper management are therefore important competencies in portfolio compilation! If the final presentation of the portfolio is to determine whether there is enough evidence to confirm competence, or to determine the grades for a GNVQ, then learners and assessors have to make judgements about whether evidence meets certain criteria, including:

- *Validity* – does the evidence accurately match the performance criteria and assess the things it claims to assess?
- *Sufficiency* – is there enough relevant evidence to infer competence across the necessary range and scope?
- *Authenticity* – is the evidence generated by the learner's own work?
- *Relevance* – is the evidence a result of recent experience, which infers that the learner can still do that particular thing?

It can be difficult for assessors to stipulate exactly how much evidence needs to be presented for particular criteria. In NVQs and GNVQs, awarding bodies provide guidelines for the frequency with which a particular criterion must be met, or the time scale over which evidence can be generated, or what proportion of a portfolio's content should be used to make a decision about grades in a GNVQ. But guidelines cannot replace the need for teachers to discuss the criteria, or for them to moderate each other's interpretations of them. It is therefore important for a programme team to discuss the acceptable range and amount of evidence, to produce exemplars and to review any external exemplars produced by awarding bodies. It can help to consider:

- whether there should be a standardized format for portfolios, eg the same order of contents, size etc;
- what is included: 'typical' direct and indirect evidence;
- the amount and scope of evidence, particularly in areas where there is a tendency towards a lack of consistency;
- opportunities for generating evidence in line with an overall assessment plan for the programme.

Stages in compiling a portfolio and record of achievement

The stages of compiling and using portfolios and records of achievement follow the assessment cycle outlined in Chapter 2.

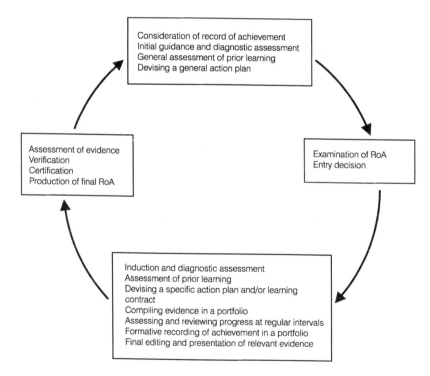

Figure 6.1 *Using records and portfolios at different stages of assessment*

Different formats for a record of achievement

At the point when a portfolio is used for deciding on the contents of a final RoA, its intended use and audience determine its format. A final RoA might consist of:

- *a simple record of units or modules* achieved as part of a whole award, which can be updated as an individual progresses through her/his learning;
- *a more detailed account of achievements* presented as a portfolio of evidence and recorded as a result of diagnostic assessment, review and action planning for a particular programme;
- *a record of progress and achievement in core skills*, which links different parts of a programme together and which includes achievements from work-based learning;
- *a combination* of these.

Planning assessment for RoAs and portfolios

Managing and implementing records of achievement is a complex process. An overall strategy for assessment and quality assurance systems enables institutions to decide how RoAs and portfolios will be used in formative and summative assessment, and to implement structures and procedures for these different purposes.

A national record of achievement

Using and maintaining the national record of achievement
A school, college, university or training organization can use school-leavers' national records as part of its initial guidance and diagnostic assessment, and as the basis for action planning. A strategy can identify how RoAs will be maintained and updated throughout a learner's programme, and how it will be used in managing modular programmes, especially where learners mix parts of A-levels, degree programmes, GNVQs and NVQs.

Good practice in using records of achievement
An assessment strategy can make a commitment to good practice in using RoAs at different stages of assessment. A strategy can promote RoAs as:

- *integral to learning process*, involving learners during initial guidance and the learning programme, and focusing on positive achievements;
- *based around clearly understood learning outcomes*, which clarify the purposes of RoAs at different stages;

- *promoting a coherent approach to planning* and implementing learning experiences by being part of an assessment plan and scheme of work;
- covering a *broad range of achievements*, such as:
  - subject-specific skills, knowledge and understanding;
  - cross-curricular experiences and core skills;
  - personal achievements and experiences;
- *providing evidence* which is capable of verification and moderation;
- *producing records and reports* readily understood by learners and different audiences for summative purposes, and also for monitoring the quality of learning programmes.

Quality assurance

Monitoring learners' achievements
An assessment strategy will need to consider how RoAs should feed into systems for monitoring learners' progress throughout a programme. A summative RoA can provide a source of qualitative and quantitative data about achievements and an important source of data for course monitoring and evaluation.

Internal verification
An institution-wide process for internal verification can consider and monitor how RoAs are used in learning programmes, and the usefulness and quality of the final product. This can also be an important mechanism for staff development in relation to RoAs.

Documentation
An assessment strategy can identify standardized formats and good practice in presenting portfolios and RoAs. Standardized documentation, as well as serving the needs of learners and external users of the RoA, can also be important for extracting data for quality assurance and programme monitoring. It also makes internal verification and moderation easier to manage.

Teachers' records
The records which teachers compile, based on the outcomes of formative and summative assessment, need to serve a variety of purposes, complementing rather than duplicating the records which learners are compiling through their RoAs and portfolios. Teachers' records can provide:

- information about the needs, attainments and speed of progress of individual learners against agreed criteria, which enables teachers to set learners' targets and appropriate learning tasks;

- information which helps teachers to modify and evaluate their schemes of work, learning activities, remedial action, resources etc;
- a basis for feedback to learners and other interested parties, such as other teachers, about learners' progress and achievements;
- a basis for contributing to an organization's evaluation of its overall performance, and groups of learners in different subject and curriculum areas;
- a process which is flexible enough to record unexpected achievements or outcomes.

Teachers' skills in using RoAs and portfolios

Reviewing progress

In addition to the administrative skills of maintaining and updating records which can serve a variety of purposes, teachers increasingly have to review and assess learners' progress in collaboration with the learners themselves. This involves subject-based teachers who might not be accustomed to a tutorial role, as well as those who are more experienced in pastoral and tutorial activities. Activities for managing reviews of progress, either in a group or one to one include:

- providing a structure and routine to the review or tutorial;
- setting time deadlines and targets for the tutorial and enabling learners to do the same;
- asking appropriate questions such as 'problem posing' and open-ended questions, and actively listening to the answers;
- managing self- and peer assessment activities and processing the outcomes;
- being familiar with the recording system and its requirements;
- developing genuine two-way communication.

Editing a portfolio

In summative reviews, where the purpose is to agree on final evidence and statements of achievement, teachers can benefit from the experience of assembling their own portfolio – something which the units of assessment for NVQs intend to provide. Familiarity with awarding body requirements greatly assist learners in assembling their final evidence.

Tensions and dilemmas

Formative and summative assessment

It is apparent from the history of the vocational curriculum that there is tension between the need to meet external requirements, and a view that time to reflect effectively on what is being learned and on strengths and weaknesses greatly enhances learning and motivation. The development of records of achievement illustrates this tension, where there has been concern in recent years that the onerous requirements of the National Curriculum, NVQs and GNVQs distort the formative and open-ended emphasis of RoAs which were promoted in early initiatives. Self-assessment and ipsative assessment in particular can be heavily steered by external requirements, especially when time and resources to support these processes are at a premium. The demands of summative assessment against extensive specifications for evidence and recording can make genuine and enjoyable learning difficult. If the process is too unwieldy and cumbersome, some educators and curriculum designers' hopes for RoAs and portfolios to be integral to learning will not be realized. In contrast, others believe that records of achievement can 'humanize' prescriptive aspects of assessment and help learners to realize that there is more to achievement than the number of units completed or a level of attainment.

An assessment policy and strategy can take account of this particular tension and contain specific educational aims. These might include a commitment to celebrating a broad range of achievements, a commitment to formative and self-assessment, and to finding ways of balancing external requirements with teachers' and learners' interpretations of these.

Creating valid and reliable assessment

When teachers are extensively involved in reviewing progress and helping learners provide evidence of achievements from life and work experiences, issues of standardization and reliability on the quality, scope and presentation of portfolios emerge. Moving from a formative to a summative role can be difficult for both teachers and learners. In an attempt to ameliorate this, some schools and colleges separate the two assessment functions by assigning them to different assessors. Others incorporate RoAs and portfolios in procedures for internal verification and moderation.

Summary

RoAs and portfolios explicitly put learners at the centre of assessment and learning processes. They are also designed to bring a wide range of skills and personal qualities and attributes into these processes. As a result, developments in this area of assessment have changed many teachers' attitudes and practices in positive ways. But the central role that RoAs and portfolios play in the vocational curriculum also illustrates some of the wider tensions which exist in all assessment regimes. Some of the dilemmas which these tensions produce can be partly resolved through staff development, discussion and moderation of assessment judgements and decisions. Others raise more fundamental issues for the whole education and training system. An assessment strategy can help organizations to consider how RoAs and portfolios fit into different aspects of a learning programme. This is dealt with in more depth in Chapter 9.

Further reading

Broadfoot, P (ed) (1986) *Profiles and Records of Achievement: A Review of Issues and Practice*, Holt, Rinehart and Winston, London.

Further Education Development Agency (1995) *Access to fair assessment: cultural and linguistic factors in assessment*, FEDA, London.

Further Education Development Agency (1993) *Managing Learning: the role of recording achievement*, FEDA, London.

Hargreaves, A (1986) 'Ideological: Record Breakers' in Broadfoot, P (1986) as above.

Stratton, N (1986) 'Recording achievement: the City and Guilds experience' in Broadfoot, P (1986) as above.

7   Assessing Knowledge, Competence and Core Skills

As the vocational curriculum becomes more extensive, the scope of learning outcomes covered by formative and summative assessment widens too. In addition to outcomes defined as important by awarding bodies and the NCVQ, subject traditions, the educational purposes and mission which an institution sets itself, the aspirations of learners and the aims of teachers all affect what is assessed. Previous chapters have shown that the scope of achievements which are deemed to be important for assessing and recording has greatly increased over the past 15 years. As well as subject knowledge, practical skills and competencies, assessment includes intellectual and cognitive skills, personal qualities and attributes, values and attitudes, interpersonal skills, problem solving, setting targets and evaluating one's own work.

Different programmes place a different emphasis on these outcomes. NVQs focus on the skills and knowledge which underpin the demonstration of practical competencies in the workplace; GNVQs cover the application of knowledge and principles to a broad occupational area and core or 'transferable' skills; vocational degrees and professional development programmes will include some of the scope of GNVQs and NVQs, and also emphasize detailed critical analysis and evaluation, a synthesis of competing perspectives or theories and use of relevant research methods. The increased scope of what is to be assessed for formative and summative purposes requires teachers to extend their repertoire of assessment methods and processes. NVQs, GNVQs, and accreditation of prior learning have had positive effects in changing our notions about what constitutes evidence of achievement, and about the ways that this can be presented and assessed.

A wider scope for assessment has fostered research and developments in records of achievement and criterion-referenced assessment. It has also led to criticism of over-assessing the recall of subject knowledge at the expense of other attributes and qualities. At the same time, NVQs have been the subject of debate about the place of 'underpinning knowledge' in practical competence. This has raised questions about whether knowledge should be assessed separately, inferred from the practical competence itself, or ignored altogether. Other debates focus on the place of 'core' and 'transferable' skills in the vocational curriculum, particularly their role in GNVQs. These issues are often controversial because they reflect different views about the purposes of education, training and assessment.

In planning a coherent assessment strategy for a programme, it is important to consider the scope of learning outcomes and appropriate methods to assess them. Assessment methods have to be used flexibly so that they assess different types of learning outcomes as reliably as possible. Consideration of progression and levels of achievement are also important. A modular curriculum makes this planning more crucial because it can help to avoid over-assessment of some outcomes at the expense of others, and ensure adequate coverage of a range of outcomes.

This chapter aims to:

● describe different learning outcomes and their associated assessment methods;
● identify the main features of assessing knowledge, core skills and competence;
● identify some of the complexities in planning assessment for these areas;
● provide some practical guidelines for planning assessment.

Classifying learning outcomes in the vocational curriculum

Even the most cursory examination of different qualifications reveals a bewildering set of terms used to describe learning outcomes, and a wide range in the types of skills and qualities they encompass. Outside generic categories, such as 'skills', 'knowledge' and 'understanding', are many others which are usually understood inside a community of teachers and assessors, but which will mean different things to outsiders.

Classifications of learning outcomes also lead to controversy about what is included in different categories. Defining what should be included in the areas of 'core' and 'transferable' skills is particularly difficult, since they cross all the categories described below.

Personal skills and qualities

The history of the vocational curriculum reveals growing political and educational interest in assessing personal skills and qualities. There is a strong belief amongst designers of qualifications, and teachers themselves, that unless these skills and qualities are explicitly defined and assessed for certification purposes, they become marginalized. Others are concerned about the validity of assessing these aspects of behaviour and learning, particularly if assessment leads to summative, public statements about a learner's personal skills and attributes. In higher education, some of these skills have been developed through attention to 'enterprise skills'. Personal skills and attributes are developed in GNVQs through core skills and are also emphasized in the grading criteria. In some initiatives, personal skills and qualities have been referred to as transferable skills.

Learning outcomes for personal skills and qualities can encompass:

- mental characteristics: openness, agility, imagination and creativity;
- attitudes and values, for example, empathy, or a commitment to anti-discriminatory behaviour;
- personality: integrity, emotional resilience, ambition, sensitivity to social responsibilities;
- leadership ability;
- a concern for quality, improvement of own learning.

Knowledge and theory

The difference between academic and vocational programmes is often delineated by referring to other learning outcomes in terms such as 'theoretical' or 'abstract' and 'practical' or 'applied'. In many programmes, learners are required to recall or describe propositional knowledge as facts, principles and relevant concepts. Quite often, this recall is not linked to a demonstration of how such knowledge applies to a practical situation or skill. In both vocational and academic subjects, if knowledge is merely recalled rather than applied to practice, it might be said to be theoretical.

In NVQs, underpinning knowledge tends to be propositional, identifying the relevant facts, procedures and, occasionally, principles which affect a particular practical skill or competence. Many programme syllabuses outline 'indicative content', which often consists of factual and propositional knowledge. Learning outcomes prefaced with terms such as 'identify', 'describe', 'list', 'name', 'record', 'state' are therefore asking learners to recall knowledge rather than apply it. As well as factual information, knowledge also encompasses judgements about particular situations or people, procedures and processes which must be followed, and actions which must be taken in different situations.

When describing certain learning outcomes, programme designers and teachers will often use knowledge synonymously with understanding. This can be confusing, since understanding encompasses some complex mental or intellectual abilities which need to be assessed differently from the recall of propositional knowledge.

Understanding and cognitive skills

When teachers and assessors talk about understanding, they are sometimes referring to the recall and replication of knowledge. More often, understanding seems to denote more sophisticated mental or cognitive abilities, such as organizing and reordering information, synthesizing different ideas and relating one idea to another, analysing ideas and information, evaluating the implications of ideas or information. At higher levels of cognitive skill, these might involve controversial or opposing ideas, and a greater degree of original or personal analysis. Understanding and cognitive skills therefore include:

- acquiring, handling, processing and storing information;
- organization, analysis, synthesis and evaluation;
- decision-making, planning and problem-solving.

Social and interpersonal skills

A wide range of social and interpersonal skills and attributes are widely viewed as important for life and occupational roles. 'Active learning' has been promoted as a desirable move away from traditional, more didactic teaching, and has made it possible for learners to practise and develop these skills. They are also included in summative assessment and accreditation in growing numbers of qualifications. Examples of social and interpersonal skills include:

- cooperation with others in group tasks or projects;
- leadership of group projects;
- negotiation of group tasks;
- interviewing peers and those in authority;
- guiding and advising peers;
- assessing the work of others.

Practical skills

In many people's minds, the vocational curriculum is synonymous with the 'practical' curriculum, where technical, technological and practical skills in designing, making and manipulating materials and objects are central to many occupational roles. In NVQs, practical skills are part of occupational competence and different contexts where they must be demonstrated are specified in the performance criteria.

Practical skills are usually accompanied both in teaching and assessment by other types of learning outcomes. There have been strong disagreements in NVQs about how the demonstration of cognitive skills and knowledge should be assessed (see *Competence*, p.111).

Values and ethics

Various attempts have been made to define the value base of different occupational roles, and also to include them for assessment purposes. Many NVQs and other professional qualifications will define learning outcomes based on certain values and ethical standpoints, and specify the criteria and contexts in which they must be assessed. In NVQ Care qualifications, for example, candidates must show a 'commitment to anti-discriminatory practice with clients', and this forms a unit of competence for assessment. Other values identified in different NVQs include:

- acknowledging clients' beliefs and identity;
- applying ethical standards or an agreed code of practice to own practice;
- maintaining confidentiality;
- communicating accurately without deception.

(Steadman *et al.*, 1994)

Core skills

Throughout the education and training system there have been numerous models of core and transferable skills. In the vocational curriculum, different definitions and approaches have emerged since the introduction of training schemes for young people, and continued through TVEI, CPVE and BTEC programmes. Interest in defining essential skills and qualities which could transcend work and life contexts, and which are therefore seen as transferable, has been tangled up with other attempts to define what should be at the 'core' of any curriculum. Sometimes, core and transferable are used simultaneously or synonymously. Different qualifications have developed their own categories of core skills, and some schools and colleges have also defined learning outcomes which they believe are core aspects of a particular institutional mission, or which define aspects of provision that learners are entitled to in any programme. Core is therefore sometimes linked to notions of entitlement: in TVEI developments, for example, personal and social education was viewed in this way.

Core skills can encompass a diverse range of concepts and viewpoints:

- Certain personal skills, attributes and qualities are transferable between situations and contexts:
  - problem solving;
  - monitoring the quality of one's own work;
  - team work and group work;

– study skills.
- Certain skills are central to the development of more specific occupational or practical skills:
  - application of number;
  - communication skills;
  - foreign languages.
- Certain skills and knowledge are central to progress in a specific subject:
  - progressing from easy to complex concepts.
- Certain skills or learning outcomes are the aim of the whole institution, and are therefore an entitlement for all learners in it:
  - personal and social education;
  - enterprise skills;
  - leisure and creative skills.

From the range of categories, it is clear that core skills – depending on how they are defined – cover personal skills and qualities (such as self-assessment, group work and the ability to work independently), some practical skills underpinned with relevant knowledge, or higher level cognitive skills such as synthesis, evaluation and critical self-reflection.

Core skills in GNVQs

Current developments which specify the core skills for GNVQs might mean that the learning outcomes specified in the core skills units could become the basis for all core skills in post-16 education and training, and in higher education. The development of core skills units in GNVQs has arisen from research by the NCVQ, which has identified a set of skills which are believed to underpin performance in a wide range of settings. They reflect an aim of previous vocational and pre-vocational initiatives, which was to enhance people's ability to perform more effectively in new and unfamiliar settings. This aim was a response to the continuous, and often stressful, change which has come to characterize the demands of many, if not all, occupational roles. Throughout the recent history of the vocational curriculum, various reports have referred to core skills as 'essential' if people are to deal effectively with continuous social and occupational change. Core skills aim to enable people to be flexible and adaptable to change. The scope of learning outcomes covered by core skills has been different in each initiative, but there have been common themes.

Early developments in core skills emphasized the idea that learners should be able to transfer skills to new situations, and that this was essential if they were to be flexible and adaptable. To a large extent, this ability to transfer skills was taken for granted. In GNVQs, core skills in communication, application of number and information technology are intended to provide learners with essential or basic skills which are common to a wide range of occupational settings. Learners' ability to show that they can use skills in diverse settings is built into the performance criteria which now specify the number and types of contexts for assessing performance.

The ability to plan, monitor and evaluate the quality of one's own learning, and to do this independently, is seen in GNVQs as an essential feature in ensuring the transferability of basic and other skills to different contexts. To achieve this, certain personal skills and qualities are also classified as core skills, appearing as 'Improving own learning and performance', which incorporates the skills of planning and setting targets and then reviewing them, and 'Working with others' which includes teamwork and collaboration. These different units are classified as mandatory or optional units:

- communication
- application of number
- information technology

  mandatory

- working with others
- improving own learning and performance

  optional

Skills in planning, monitoring and evaluating the quality of one's own work underpins the grading criteria for merit or distinction in GNVQs. This has elevated the concept of 'learning how to learn' as central in helping people learn more quickly and confidently in new situations.

Assessing core skills

A large number of schools and colleges use the two optional units as core skills in other programmes, such as GCE A levels and NVQs. Managing the incorporation of core skills into the vocational curriculum, and ensuring they are coherently assessed, has not been easy. Changes have been made to the core skills specifications and more guidance has been given to schools and colleges. Guidelines from awarding bodies, the FEDA and the NCVQ, stress the importance of 'auditing' and 'mapping' where there will be opportunities for learners to practise and develop them, and where – and how – they will be assessed. The overall picture of where and how core skills will appear in a programme is important, and this can be linked to an assessment plan.

Colleges and schools have adopted different strategies for assessing core skills, including:

- integrating them with vocational subject areas, with teaching and assessing carried out by vocational specialists or between vocational and core specialists working together;
- offering them in specialist core workshops or sessions, and linking them to the way in which core skills appear in assignments and projects;
- offering them through flexible studypacks and workshops;
- recording them in separate core skills 'logs';
- identifying them from other projects and assignments and cross-referencing to the specifications of evidence and criteria.

Different assessment methods

Some core skills aim to foster learners' deep rather than surface engagement with the learning process. A *deep* approach emphasizes intrinsic motivation and enjoyment in learning, relating different tasks to personal experience and making connections between seemingly disparate aspects of learning. A *surface* approach, on the other hand, relies on getting through the requirements, memorizing without understanding in order to achieve a task, and not connecting learning to personal experience. The idea of transferability of learning is linked to the notion of deep learning, whereas short-term recall is associated with more surface approaches. Assessment of problem solving and the use of self- and peer assessment therefore has to encourage:

- acquiring and practising skills in a wide range of contexts;
- using practical examples, followed by underpinning knowledge and concepts;
- requiring learners to adopt a holistic approach to problem solving rather than breaking it down into artificial or separate elements;
- encouraging reflection on own learning styles and effective and ineffective approaches to learning;
- making links with the uses of diagnostic assessment outlined in Chapter 4.

A range of methods can be used to assess core skills, and can be linked to the stages of the assessment cycle outlined in Chapter 2, covering initial diagnostic assessment, formative feedback about progress, and summative assessment. The chart in Figure 7.1 (p.118) shows the range of assessments which can be used for different types of learning outcome.

Competence

The impact of NVQs

The development of national standards of occupational competence in NVQs has had an enormous impact on the way that we view 'evidence', 'performance' and 'underpinning knowledge'. Debates about NVQs' influence in these areas have been fierce, and this section cannot adequately summarize all the technical and educational issues which have been covered. Supporters of NVQs have been extremely critical of past practices in assessment, particularly the distortions caused by rank ordering and selection, and the lack of specificity about the range of situations and contexts in which people should demonstrate their competence.

NVQs have promoted much wider access to assessment and accreditation, and the idea of mastery across all the criteria which make up successful performance. To gain a unit of competence, a learner must show sufficient evidence of all elements of competence in the unit against the performance criteria. The other impact of NVQs has been to separate assessment of evidence from the need to gain evidence through a specified learning programme: in NVQs, evidence can come from any life and educational experience provided it demonstrates competence.

Critics of early versions of NVQs questioned whether knowledge and understanding needed to be assessed separately rather than inferred through practical competence. There have also been concerns about whether very detailed specifications of criteria could adequately standardize assessors' judgements across different contexts, such as the workplace and colleges. Other criticisms have been made of the bureaucracy which accompanies assessment against detailed specifications, and the reduction of complex tasks into isolated elements.

Assessing competence

NVQs' definitions and specifications of competence require learners to perform at the same standard as that expected from other employees doing the same job. From the earliest developments in NVQs, competence has been promoted as a broad concept. It is the ability to perform a range of tasks or jobs in a range of situations and contexts and under different, real life conditions. This concept embodies openness to change, adaptability, motivation and a commitment to improving one's own performance. It includes interpersonal skills, task and people management, supervising and working with others, adopting appropriate values and knowing how performance might be transferred to other situations.

Assessment in NVQs judges whether an individual can or cannot demonstrate their ability to meet the standard of competence laid down in the specifications. These indicate detailed criteria, the range of contexts and situations which must be covered, and the scope of particular tasks. They also indicate types of evidence and any underpinning knowledge. As a result, NVQs have changed expectations amongst assessors, teachers and learners about how to use criteria. Instead of assessors basing their judgements on their own interpretations, they now use detailed external specifications, and learners have equal access to these criteria and can use them to identify and collect evidence.

NVQs' definitions of competence have also affected the type of evidence which is seen to be suitable for assessment. There is a strong emphasis on assessment in real working situations based on normal, everyday work performance as far as possible. However, when this is not possible, situations can be set up for the specific purposes of assessment, as simulations or tests.

Performance can be supplemented by assessment of knowledge and understanding to find out what someone would do in a different situation. Evidence can come directly from learners' performance at work or in simulations of work activities, through observing what they do, artefacts they have made, reports and written accounts, videos of different activities. Indirect and supplementary evidence includes answers to tests of knowledge and understanding, self-assessments, written accounts of what learners would do in a different situation, testimonials or comments by employers, colleagues, customers and clients and other forms of references. In many cases, assessors will have to combine their judgements with other assessors, such as workplace supervisors, line managers, and other teachers.

Knowledge and understanding

It is common in course rationales and definitions of learning outcomes to use terms such as knowledge and understanding interchangeably or synonymously. However, in clarifying more precisely what is to be assessed and how it will be done, it is helpful to differentiate between the two terms. Assessment of knowledge involves testing someone's ability to recall facts, and relevant principles. 'Understanding' involves more complex cognitive abilities such as the ability to apply knowledge to a real life or hypothetical context. Understanding may also require learners to present what they have done in a coherent way.

Once assessment goes beyond the testing of propositional knowledge by recalling facts and information, higher level cognitive skills involve the application of knowledge to practice. Learners may have to make connections between different ideas or to synthesize them in more complex ways.

They might have to present a synopsis or synthesis of other people's arguments, analyse their implications, or reveal the implicit assumptions behind them. Other cognitive abilities are tested when learners have to evaluate the implications of completely opposing viewpoints or analyse controversial or complex ideas. Evaluating other people's criticisms of ideas, or criticising ideas from their own viewpoint, and convincing an external audience of the coherence of this criticism assesses other, related abilities.

Different cognitive skills

Knowledge and understanding range from the random guesswork which some learners bring to multiple choice tests, to sophisticated or original analyses of complex practices and their underpinning concepts and theories. When *understand* appears in a learning outcome, it can mean recall of knowledge or other cognitive abilities and it is therefore worth trying to be more precise when using it. Bloom's taxonomy of cognitive objectives is useful for defining understanding more precisely, and although his idea that there is a hierarchy of skills has been criticised, the terms themselves, and the abilities they describe, are useful. The following descriptions are drawn from Bloom (1956).

Knowledge
1. *Knowledge of specifics*
- recall of specific or isolated bits of information;
- knowledge of terminology and definitions;
- knowledge of specific facts and information.
2. *Knowledge of ways and means for dealing with specifics:*
- knowledge of conventions, eg the rules of punctuation;
- knowledge of trends and sequences.

Comprehension
1. *Translation:*
- translation from one level of abstraction to another, eg translate a lengthy part of a communication to a briefer, more abstract version;
- translation from one symbolic form to another, eg read musical scores;
- translation from one verbal form to another, eg foreign languages to English.
2. *Interpretation:*
- eg comprehend and interpret various types of reading material with increasing clarity and depth;
- eg interpret various types of data.

3. *Extrapolation:*
- The ability to make sense of something and apply the ideas to new problems or situations, eg predict consequences of action or draw conclusions.

Application

This covers the ability to use a theory or information in a new situation without being directed to solve a particular problem, eg apply principles to identify the relevant characteristics in a new situation.

Analysis

This covers the breakdown of materials into constituent parts, showing how they relate to each other and how they are organized:

- analysis of elements, eg recognize unstated assumptions;
- analysis of relationships, eg distinguish relevant from irrelevant statements in an argument;
- analysis of organizational principles, eg recognize techniques used in advertising or political rhetoric.

Synthesis

This is the ability to work with different elements and combine them in ways which create a new pattern or structure:

- production of a unique communication, eg make an effective speech or organize ideas coherently in writing;
- production of a plan or procedure, eg plan a programme of assessment.

Evaluation

This is the ability to construct an argument, compare opposing arguments and make judgements and draw conclusions.

Assessing knowledge and understanding

In planning assessment of knowledge or cognitive skills, it is important to carefully define the intended learning outcomes and criteria which indicate the expected range of ideas and knowledge which should or could be presented and the type of evidence which will demonstrate these. The example below is taken from GNVQ Communication core skills level 1.

Produce written material
Performance criteria:

- include information which is accurate and relevant to the subject;
- check that text is legible and the meaning is clear;
- follow appropriate standard conventions;
- present information in a format that suits the audience and purpose.

Range:

- Subject: straightforward.
- Conventions: spelling, punctuation.
- Format: pre-set, outline.
- Audience: people familiar with subject and who know the student.

Evidence indicators:

- At least four pieces of material on straightforward subjects.
- Two pieces written in different outline formats.
- All materials should be accurate, complete and relevant to the subject and purpose and should comply with standard conventions.
- At least one piece should be hand-written.

Guidance is given in the specifications for the type of assessment activities which might be appropriate.

(NCVQ, 1995)

(NB Not all evidence indicators and specifications for interpreting them have been included in this example.)

It is clear from the example above that the outcomes and criteria for assessing them could easily appear at a variety of levels in the vocational curriculum. A specification for assessment therefore needs to be interpreted in the context of the particular programme for which it is designed. Standards of performance also need, as other chapters have argued, to be discussed and shared between teachers and learners.

Assessing knowledge seems fairly straight forward, but it becomes more complex as soon as the learning outcomes move away from factual recall and identification of relevant knowledge. A range of methods for assessing knowledge includes:

- multiple choice questions;
- oral or written question and answer;
- true/false questions;
- 'matching block' questions;

- descriptive accounts.

Methods of assessing the cognitive skills of comprehension, synthesis, evaluation and analysis include:

- essays and reports;
- book reviews;
- interviews;
- oral presentations;
- carefully designed questions and answers, and multiple choice questions can also be used to assess some cognitive skills.

It is common for teachers to assume they are assessing higher level cognitive skills when the assessment method actually assesses knowledge recall and memorization. Rowntree (1987) cites research which shows that in the 1960s, 80% of A level and 40% of university final questions could be answered by memorization. In a recent project in higher education, UDACE found that lecturers frequently defined learning outcomes in higher order skills, but used examination and essay questions which did not test these (UDACE, 1992). It is therefore useful to:

- differentiate clearly between knowledge and other cognitive skills;
- identify which aspects will be assessed and which method is appropriate;
- identify criteria for the range and level of evidence which will be appropriate;
- produce an assessment plan to show where different skills will be covered.

Carrying out an assessment

All assessments incorporate the same processes of planning, identifying the right method, collecting evidence, making judgements and giving feedback.

Assessment preparation includes:

- planning how assessment will take place across a programme;
- establishing a large bank of assessment activities for different purposes;
- developing a programme portfolio of exemplars from learners' previous work, to help teachers develop a shared sense of standards in their programme and to teach learners how to use the criteria and assess the quality of their work;
- identifying the reason for assessment, the learning outcomes it covers and the appropriate methods to use.

Identifying the right method includes:

- considering the range of evidence and the possible sources which can be used, including *typical* evidence which might come from previous learning;
- making sure learners understand the purpose of the assessment, what they have to do and how they will be assessed.

Collecting and assessing evidence includes:

- assessing evidence and recording judgements, helpful and constructive formative comments for individuals and groups, which may also help a group recognize common strengths and weaknesses;
- making judgements as objectively as possible.

Communicating the outcomes and implications includes:

- providing constructive and specific feedback, both to groups and to individuals, which helps them to improve next time;
- passing on appropriate information to others, such as needs for learning support identified through initial diagnostic assessment, or new needs identified during a programme.

Figure 7.1 indicates the range of assessment methods available for assessing different types of learning outcomes.

Summary

A wide range of skills, attributes and personal qualities are assessed in the vocational curriculum. Precision in the types of learning outcomes which are defined, and in the criteria which are used to assess them can help in planning coherent assessment. Mapping the different learning outcomes and deciding which methods should be used enables a variety and balance of approaches to be used.

ASSESSMENT METHODS

LEARNING OUTCOMES	METHOD	FEATURES	ISSUES	CRITERIA
Knowledge – recall and replication	Checklists Questions and answers Multiple choice questions True/false questions Factual reports	Can be defined by awarding bodies/teachers/learners	Easy to administer and mark Can be refined and improved by experienced test designers	Define expected range of key terms 'State/describe key terms and concepts'
Personal skills – monitoring and evaluating quality of own work	Reflective logs/journals Self-assessment Peer assessment Tutorial review Ipsative assessment Contracts/action plans Profile grids Others' testimonials	Can be designed by teachers/learners/awarding bodies Criteria are given for assessing the contexts and range of situations where these should be demonstrated GNVQ specifications Includes scope for using other's testimonials of a learner's skills	Validity can be difficult, eg transferability of the skill cannot be assumed Need for internal moderation Need for clear criteria and evidence required	Range of complex or simple activities Independent activity Organizing and starting own work Monitor own progress systematically and thoroughly identify sources of information Use of 'standard' sources of information, or original or more inaccessible ones
– working with others	Teacher/assessor observation Peer assessment Reflective 'logs'/journals Profile grids Rating schedules Task groups Presentations Audio/visual records	Peer and self-assessment can be more valid than a teacher's assessment Learners need to be 'taught' how to use peer and self-assessment	As above in 'monitoring and evaluating quality of own work' Transferability may be heavily dependent on personal and contextual factors	Differentiation of who learners have to work with, eg known/unknown, in authority/peers Complexity of task and context

Cognitive skills – synthesis – analysis – critical evaluation – organizing complex information – application of theory to practice	Essays Reports/projects Interviews Question and answer Open book tests Book reviews	Can be designed by teachers and awarding bodies, and learners at a certain stage of their learning	Reliability requires moderation and discussion of criteria Degree of originality required by criteria needs to be discussed Exemplars of required standard Levels of learning programme affect expectations of criteria	Clarity of argument Logical presentation An obvious or expected synthesis or an original one Straightforward or complex ideas Range of expected or new ideas
Practical skills – making and producing things – manipulating materials and objects	Observation – in person or by video Micro tasks (smaller components assessed separately and built up over time) Check lists Practical tests Progress sheets	Can incorporate artefacts made in other contexts Might involve assessment by different assessors, eg workplace supervisors, colleagues etc, as well as teachers Direct and indirect evidence	Assessment increasingly involves workplace assessors and joint assessment decisions. Criteria need to be discussed among assessors	Range and scope of practical skills are specified Simplicity or complexity of materials Working to time scales and deadlines
Attitudes, qualities and values – reflection on practice – leadership – commitment to equal opportunities – concern for quality	Reflective 'logs' or journals Question and answer Essays Observation Third party endorsements Case studies and simulations	Contextual features and issues need careful definition	Raises problems of validity and reliability Problems of subjectivity or controversy in which values and attitudes are defined and assessed	Details of codes of practice Context and client expectations

Figure 7.1 Assessment methods

Further reading

Bloom, B (1956) *A Taxonomy of Educational Objectives: Cognitive Domain*, Mckay, New York.

Jessup, G (1990) *Outcomes: NVQs and the emerging model of education and training*, Falmer Press, London.

Hyland, T (1994) *Competence, Education and NVQs*, Cassell, London.

NCVQ (1995) *Core Skills Units in: Application of number*, Communication and Information Technology Level 1, NCVQ, London.

Rowntree, D (1987) *Assessing Students: How shall we know them?* Kogan Page, London.

Steadman, S, *et al* (1994) *Ethics in Occupational Standards*, NVQs and SVQs, Report No 22, Employment Department, Sheffield.

UDACE (1992) *Learning Outcomes in Higher Education*, FEDA, London.

Wolf, A (1995) *Competence Based Assessment*, Open University Press, Buckingham.

8 Developing Professional Expertise in Assessment

Given the technical complexity of assessment and its social and educational importance, it is not surprising that many managers and teachers – and learners – find assessment a difficult process. Recent reports from the FEFC Inspectorate, Employment Department and FEDA reinforce evidence from teachers' and learners' everyday experiences about the difficulties of carrying out positive, supportive and useful assessment. Some of these are new difficulties, caused by the very specific requirements of NVQs and GNVQs. Others illustrate long-running tensions and dilemmas in assessment, highlighted throughout this book.

Teachers play an increasingly important role in assessment. They interpret detailed specifications and requirements for formative and summative assessment and have to share their understanding of these with learners and colleagues. Gipps (1995) shows that teachers' skills, knowledge and commitment are crucial for the quality of assessment:

> 'any assessment model, policy or programme will only be as good as the teachers who use it: devalue the role of teachers and deprofessionalize their training and no assessment technology will replace their skill. It is teachers who teach the concepts and skills, prepare [students] for the assessments, feedback... and move learners in the right direction. To limit the role of teachers in assessment would be the ultimate misconstrual of the process of teaching and learning'.

Yet time to acquire a good understanding of purposes, methods and the requirements of different awarding bodies is increasingly at a premium. Creating common understandings cannot, therefore, only be achieved by giving teachers tighter and more detailed specifications to work with. Somehow, opportunities for professional development in which teachers take part in order to enhance their knowledge and skills in assessment, have to balance these specifications with a deeper understanding. Wolf (1993) argues that:

> 'In seeking to improve the assessment methods they employ teachers and lecturers welcome practical guidance but practical guidance can be of limited value if it becomes detached from an understanding of the principles, potential and limitations of the theoretical model.'

Staff development and training can enable teachers to use assessment positively and efficiently by identifying and sharing good practice. Staff development can also help teachers and managers clarify which assessment problems are the result of poor practice, which are the result of poor design, and which stem from the fundamental tensions which surround any assessment. Teachers will need to consider their practical competencies and relevant knowledge, as well as the ways in which they construct their own individual interpretations of assessment. Critical, systematic inquiry into policy and practice in assessment, as well as gaining assessment skills and learning the requirements of assessment systems, are all important. Perhaps most crucially of all, teachers need skills in formative assessment, since this is the only aspect which improves teaching and learning (Gipps, 1995).

Staff development, therefore, covers a wide range of issues. This chapter aims to:

- identify some of the processes which enable teachers to develop their expertise and understanding in assessment;
- outline skills, knowledge and understanding which teachers need in order to be effective assessors;
- highlight the importance of recognizing different types of bias in assessment.

Influences on teachers' assessment practice

Observing how teachers assess raises some important issues for the way they implement and interpret different requirements. These can illuminate good practice to build on and share with others, and bad practice which can be tackled through staff development.

Teachers learn how to assess in a variety of ways. They are as much influenced by their colleagues, the particular requirements of a qualification and the need to make sense of the system they are using, as by anything they learn from teacher training courses or books. Research into assessment in GNVQs and NVQs carried out by various government bodies and educational researchers, and into the National Curriculum by researchers at the Institute of Education (Gipps, 1995), can be extremely illuminating for teachers who want or need to improve their assessment skills, and for those charged with helping them do this. Three important features are outlined here.

How teachers view assessment

'You often know just by looking at a piece of work what mark it should get, before you start looking at it in detail.' (school teacher)

Teachers have an internalized model of assessment which affects their assessment practice. Wolf argues that this is developed through assessment systems which teachers have previously used, and their own previous experience of being assessed. However, they are not always aware of this internalized 'model', or how it affects their attitudes to assessment and the way that they carry it out. Their ability to apply grading criteria consistently, for example, might be drawn from other experiences, such as in BTEC programmes or GCE A levels. It is also often influenced by how much common ground there is between their own interpretations and those of their colleagues. Wolf observes that assessors have a mental model of quality which they have internalized over time and which they tend to apply irrespective of written instructions or guidance. This internalized model will be particularly powerful when they are required to 'learn' a new assessment system.

> 'We spend quite a bit of time looking at each other's grades to see if they compare across the team. We don't get any time to do this, we just do it over a cup of coffee. It's a lot easier than wading through all the criteria in the guidance we get.' (school teacher)

Existing individual and group norms and standards for assessment evolve over time, often informally. Wolf (1993) argues that they can exert more influence on teachers' judgements than the criteria themselves, or the degree of ease or difficulty in using them. There are useful lessons to be learned from the way that teachers assess in other systems, especially when these are from other traditions and subject areas. Vocational assessors can therefore learn a great deal from assessment in GCSEs and A levels, and vice versa. Wolf (1993) points out that although A level outcomes are criticised for being 'loose', marker reliability is fairly high because of the way in which teachers and assessors for A levels are 'socialized' through the use of exemplars. Exemplars, and opportunities for teachers to share and discuss their judgements, are important aspects of developing professional expertise. They have enormous potential for introducing reliability and consistency of judgements into criterion-based assessment schemes and modular programmes.

Compensating for the criteria

> 'He was having a really difficult time doing the task. Normally, he can do it with his eyes shut! As well as that, he had to use a new machine from the one he normally works on. It must have been a one-off bad performance so I passed him anyway.' (college lecturer)

In her research into assessment practices in NVQs and the National Curriculum, Wolf (1993) found that in spite of being expected to apply strict criteria, teachers often use a process of 'compensating'. This process is largely subconscious, and it takes account of the context of the performance and its particular characteristics. This enables teachers to make allowances for whether a question or task was especially difficult. The more complex the behaviour being assessed, the more this happens. Assessment systems vary in the degree to which they require teachers to make complex judgements. However, the way that teachers compensate in order to make these judgements is common in all assessment systems.

To illustrate this process, Wolf (1993) uses the apparently straightforward example of assessing learners' ability to transcribe something from a manuscript. If it is complex, unreadable or merely untidy, for example, the learner may miss data or make other mistakes. There might be a criterion which requires 100% accuracy, but teachers will still tend to compensate for mistakes according to the complexity of the task or an unfamiliar context. If a learner makes mistakes because of these unfamiliar factors, then teachers will interpret a criterion more liberally. Similarly, the well-known 'halo effect' will often lead teachers to make compensations if a normally competent learner appears to perform in an uncharacteristically poor way. Like other traits in assessment, teachers are often unaware of the degree to which they are compensating, or how they make allowances for what they know (or think they know!) about candidates and the context of performance.

The difficulty is that unless these traits are discussed openly amongst teachers, there may be very wide discrepancies between teachers' interpretations. Different types of bias about candidates are likely to affect the assessor's judgements. Wolf (1993) points out that in compensating, there can be a fine line between 'justified interpretation' and 'unjustified prejudice'.

Using other criteria

> 'I give good grades for presentation and knock marks off for bad spelling and sloppy English.' (college lecturer)

Teachers' feedback on learners' work shows that they often subconsciously use criteria other than those which might be specified. In assessing practical competence, for example, a learner's linguistic ability or their general confidence may lead an assessor to make inferences about their practical skills. In assessing the quality of an argument through writing, the presentation of work can lead to negative or positive judgements about the content. The intrusion of other criteria is particularly influential in interpersonal methods of assessment where cultural, class and gender backgrounds of both assessors and learners can affect the assessment.

Although these traits cannot be eliminated from the assessment process entirely, certain practices can help to counteract them. The next section outlines some of these.

Improving assessment practice

Becoming familiar with a new system

'I feel completely disempowered by GNVQs. I've been assessing for years and I don't know what I'm doing anymore. All this recording – it takes away your professional judgements and makes you feel that you can't be trusted' (college lecturer)

Teachers are more likely to use assessment in positive and educational ways when they are involved in designing and generating assessments, discussing the standards, deciding how to get the best performance from learners, discussing their interpretation of the criteria, and developing and refining exemplars. The more they are able to do this, the less likely it is that they will see themselves as technicians carrying out an imposed curriculum and testing programme

It seems inevitable that staff development is particularly important when teachers are new to a particular programme or assessment system. Induction, opportunities for staff development, and time to work with colleagues are important for developing a shared sense of standards to pass on to learners, and consistency in interpreting the criteria. This appears to be true even when teachers are fairly experienced in other assessment systems. There is evidence from teachers' experience of the National Curriculum, the ways in which bodies like the Open College Networks operate and best practice in GCE A-levels, GCSEs, GNVQs and university assessment, that some processes enhance teachers' understanding of 'quality' and 'standards' in a particular system. These processes are summarized below:

- *Active involvement in processes* to moderate each others' assessments with networks of assessors, teachers and verifiers, and where supportive and open exploration of anomalies, similarities and disagreements can take place.
- *Developing exemplars* which give a clear indicator of the standards which learners are aiming for, and which are accompanied by discussion amongst teachers about how they were interpreted and judged.
- *Defining learning outcomes and criteria to assess them* so that teachers are better able to interpret those defined by external bodies.
- *Receiving advice and support* from awarding body verifiers and examiners.
- *Allocating mentors* to teachers new to a particular assessment regime (including experienced teachers who might be moving into a new programme).
- *Appointing assessment coordinators* to relate issues and good practice from different systems.

Sharing and discussing criteria

Other processes enhance teachers' consistency in interpreting criteria. To counteract the tendency to compensate subconsciously for certain aspects of someone's performance or for the context of assessment, clarity is needed about what can be legitimately compensated for and what cannot. Wolf (1993) argues that the process of agreeing these rules embodies decisions about what is crucial and what is optional, and the relative weight which can be given to these. Without this, an over-reliance on the specifications will lead, according to Wolf (1993), to some extreme, and therefore unacceptable, variations in interpretations.

Internal verification and moderation

'Our verifier says that there's nothing wrong with our standards.' (college curriculum manager)

As awarding bodies move towards a system of checking procedures and systems rather than moderating teachers' judgements and assessment processes, internal systems for verification will become more important if teachers are to assure the standards and quality of assessment decisions. Specific moderation of areas where criteria seem to cause confusion, disagreement or difficulty, is also important as part of an internal verification system which requires teachers to take part in informal and formal procedures for sampling assessment decisions.

For many schools, colleges and universities, a strong system of internal verification has not been a traditional feature in enhancing the quality of assessment. It is not often funded from institutional budgets. But internal verification can play a crucial role in staff development, rather than solely as a system to meet external requirements. The processes of verifying and moderating assessment decisions can be a very powerful source of support and learning about assessment. Using them for developing professional expertise can make an important contribution to quality assurance. (Chapter 4 has more information about internal verification.)

Current approaches to staff development

A range of opportunities exists for developing teachers' skills and understanding in assessment. However, it is rare for them to be coordinated in order to provide coherent progression in skills and understanding. Positive uses can be made of different types of opportunity for staff development. For staff in schools, sixth form colleges and universities, different teacher training and education programmes, and opportunities for in-service training or study can be useful sources for initial awareness raising and more in-depth updating.

Initial teacher training

The City and Guilds Further and Adult Education Certificate contains the units of assessment required to assess NVQs (these are discussed in more detail below).

The Certificate in Education for Further Education has modules on assessment, some of which also incorporate the NVQ assessor awards.

BA Teacher Education programmes also incorporate competencies in assessment, as well as consideration of wider issues and underpinning knowledge.

In-service programmes

Increasing numbers of college and school teachers undertake further professional study, and many decide to carry out action research into assessment as part of a BA or Masters degree. Some academic programmes offer modules in assessment, and these can provide an invaluable opportunity to acquire in-depth knowledge and skills in assessment, backed up by research.

In-house staff development

In response to requirements from the NCVQ that assessors in NVQ and GNVQ programmes should gain units of competence in assessment and verification, and experience these processes themselves, many colleges have devoted staff development time and budgets to programmes to provide these units. Reports vary greatly about how far the process of undertaking the NVQ units enables teachers to be better assessors.

Although there has not yet been a formal evaluation of the assessor awards, they have had some positive effects when they have been used to enable staff to reflect on the process of compiling a portfolio of evidence of competence in assessment. Some teachers say that they have broadened their perceptions about what constitutes evidence, and their repertoire of assessment methods. As part of a framework for training and staff development, the NVQ units can be a useful addition to staff updating.

Some colleges and schools have used other strategies for enhancing staff development, including:

- Lunch-time seminars on assessment issues and practice, with interesting titles!

- Cross-institution groups for different developments, such as work-based assessment, core skills, records of achievement.
- Offering staff the opportunity to put together a portfolio, showing evidence of professional development, to enable them to experience the process and accrediting this towards a BA or Masters' degree.
- Appointing mentors in assessment for new staff.
- Bringing together a cross-college group to develop an assessment policy and strategies, and accrediting the outcomes towards a BA or Master's degree.

Crucial competencies, knowledge and understanding

'Teachers were being asked to train themselves, to alter their practices, but without a shared reality.' (Fullan, 1989)
'I've been teaching for ten years. Why should I have to get this assessor's award?' (college lecturer)

Planning staff development activities requires an overview of different assessment activities, the skills that teachers need to carry them out, and the basic propositional knowledge they need to make sense of what they have to. However, for a deeper understanding and an appreciation of the wider issues which make assessment more complex than it first appears, some principles and theories are also important. The following charts incorporate competencies from the NVQ and GNVQ units of competence.

Recognizing bias

Assessment processes, and the documentation to support them, are always partial and subjective to some extent. Targets and outcomes which are included in the assessment, and those which are excluded in teachers' and assessors' interpretation of evidence, are prone to this partiality. The widespread use of portfolios and records of achievement have highlighted this dimension of assessment in particular ways, since both these rely heavily on assessing diverse evidence of achievements and processes which involve interaction between learners and assessors. However, diagnostic assessment also relies on dialogue and good relationships between teachers and learners. The difference between legitimate different treatment, and the unfair effects of bias in assessment, therefore becomes crucial in new forms of assessment.

Figure 8.1 Professional skill and knowledge in assessment

ASSESSMENT ACTIVITY	PROPOSITIONAL KNOWLEDGE	SKILLS	PRINCIPLES/ THEORIES	WIDER ISSUES
Incorporate formative and diagnostic assessment into teaching and tutorial activities	Define: – formative assessment – diagnostic assessment – summative assessment	Consider timings for informal and formal diagnostic and formative assessment	Role of diagnostic and formative assessment in teaching and learning processes	Possible 'blurring' with summative assessment Growing interest in role of diagnostic feedback
	Identify different timings for these types of assessment: – pre-course – selection – pre-module/induction – on-course – exit	Use different types of feedback Teach learners about formative/diagnostic assessment	Difference between type of feedback which improves learning and feedback which does not Theories about assessment in learning (eg Chapter 5)	Pressures of time, resources and external requirements
	Identify activities: – diagnostic tests – informal processes in class, tutorials etc.	Use observation and questioning to diagnose barriers to learning Develop exemplars		
	Identify purpose of oral and written feedback	Teach learners about purposes and processes of assessment, including peer and self-assessment		

Figure 8.1 (continued)

ASSESSMENT ACTIVITY	PROPOSITIONAL KNOWLEDGE	SKILLS	PRINCIPLES/ THEORIES	WIDER ISSUES
Share and moderate judgements with colleagues and representatives of awarding bodies	Identify awarding body requirements	Keeping administrative records, details of problem areas, etc.	How reliability and validity aim to standardize assessment	Tensions between the two processes
Ensure the consistency of assessment decisions and record the outcomes ('G' unit)	Know institutions guidelines and recording systems, staff responsibilities and roles, including own	Contributing to moderation meetings and informal discussion about standards, criteria, etc.	Historical evolution of processes which aim to standardize assessment	
	Define: – verification – moderation – validation – standardization		Difference (and overlap) between verification and moderation	
	Know grading criteria for GNVQs, degree classifications, NVQs			
	Identify timing and documentation			

ASSESSMENT ACTIVITY	PROPOSITIONAL KNOWLEDGE	SKILLS	PRINCIPLES/ THEORIES	WIDER ISSUES
Assess diverse evidence	Different types, amount and range of evidence	Deciding what sources of evidence can be used	The role of criterion-referencing in drawing up the specifications	Pros and cons of criterion-referenced assessment
	Procedures for establishing: – required amount – authenticity – validity	Making judgements about whether the learner's performance meets the criteria	Purposes of aiming for validity Procedures for obtaining validity	Balance between external specifications and moderation with colleagues
	Identifying opportunities for collecting evidence	Providing constructive and relevant feedback about strengths and weaknesses	Implications of context, inter-personal relationships, cultural issues, for learner's performance	Awareness of allowable and non-allowable compensation in making judgements
		Share and discuss judgements with colleagues, internal verifiers and external verifiers		Potential for social and cultural bias

Figure 8.1 (continued)

ASSESSMENT ACTIVITY	PROPOSITIONAL KNOWLEDGE	SKILLS	PRINCIPLES/ THEORIES	WIDER ISSUES
Devise an assessment plan which shows learners, colleagues and external verifiers or examiners: – *assessment activities* for learners to gain evidence for different parts of the programme – *timing and pace* of assessment – *formative and summative processes*	Identify the role of formative and summative assessment during the programme Describe contents and scope of an assessment plan Identify different activities: – setting assignment deadlines – marking – feedback – review – recording achievements Define: – types of unit; ie mandatory or core – grading criteria in GNVQs/degrees – the components of an assessment plan: – methods of assessment – individual schedules – review and recording procedures	Relate assessment activities to different parts of the programme: – vocational skills – core skills Negotiate assessment plans for individual learners Relate own role in plan to that of colleagues Be able to communicate plan and methods of assessment to learners Devise criteria for adequate amounts of assessment	Differentiate between formative/summative assessment Recognise dangers of over-assessment	Resources and time to implement a realistic plan

ASSESSMENT ACTIVITY	PROPOSITIONAL KNOWLEDGE	SKILLS	PRINCIPLES/ THEORIES	WIDER ISSUES
Design and administer tests for formative, diagnostic and summative assessment	Define/recognise a wide range of tests and their uses: – anecdotal methods – assignments and projects – case studies – competence-based tests – continuous summative assessment – collaborative – entry tests – essays/reports – multiple choice tests – matching block – profiles – oral tests – occupational tests – peer assessment – rating scales – self-assessment – short answer items – true/false items – aptitude tests Define terms: – criterion-referenced – ipsative – norm-referenced – criteria – evidence – range	Choose appropriate tests for a particular purpose Write tests Pilot and modify tests Prepare marking schemes and criteria Mark and grade learners' work Discuss methods and purposes with learners and colleagues Moderate judgements with colleagues	Norm and criterion referencing in assessment design Validity and reliability Formative/summative and diagnostic purposes for assessment	Historical evolution of the main features of assessment Validity and reliability Tension between these features

133

A report by the Further Education Development Agency argues that:

'Written examinations, for several generations, have disadvantaged those students who, often for reasons of class or racial origin, could express their abilities more effectively through oral communication or practical demonstration. The new [assessment] regimes use a wide variety of methods of assessment, requiring understanding of complex instructions, individual initiative, group interaction, and confidence in oral expression. These methods can further disadvantage certain groups of students... Assessors also are not neutral. They are human beings, with specific cultural backgrounds, special interests and prejudices... new... assessment regimes depend to a far greater extent than previously on a close working relationship between learner and assessor. They make demands on the assessor as communicator, as a decision-maker and as a neutral arbiter of competence.' (FEDA, 1995)

Documentation

Materials designed for assessment are potentially prone to explicit and implicit bias. Some assignment instructions and teacher explanations may assume shared understandings of assessment tasks, career paths and occupational areas which not all learners share. In preparing and monitoring documentation, FEDA (1995) highlights useful features which minimize possibilities of bias for certain groups of learners, and which make documentation more accessible for all learners. These include:

- *Using standard patterns of spoken English* rather than the written discourses and jargon of assessment, and of individual academic and vocational subjects, and avoiding inconsistency in patterns of language use.
- *Using active rather than passive forms*, and avoiding complicated, structurally difficult sentences with multiple clauses.
- *Avoiding materials which assume a particular background* in terms of ethnic, gender or class experiences.
- *Providing appropriate alternatives* or options which allow students from different backgrounds to display their specific skills and knowledge.
- *Checking that activities do not contain elements which are not acceptable* to particular groups of learners.

Interpersonal assessment

Interpersonal communication for many assessment processes means that factors in teachers' and learners' backgrounds, attitudes and experiences can affect the quality of a learner's performance. Some competencies or learning outcomes, for example, have implicit requirements for higher order language skills, where learners need to use a wide range of language registers and styles. Oral questioning is especially prone to cultural stereotypes and the use of implicit criteria, although teachers are usually unaware of how these factors affect their judgements. Verbal and non-verbal cues may be given differently to some learners than others, or different judgements might be made about linguistic ability. For example, when learners are asked about their ability to transfer experience and competence to other situations, the ease with which they can reflect, explain and infer what they might do in different circumstances is enhanced if they can do it in their first language.

Other factors are important in interpersonal approaches to assessment, for instance cultural, linguistic, class and gender background and expectations affect how easy it is for someone to reflect and explain what they are able to do and what they have or have not achieved. It is common for assessors, for example, to believe they are assessing a practical skill, but to subconsciously make judgements about the quality of performance according to a learner's linguistic fluency and confidence and cultural knowledge. Yet these factors may actually be irrelevant for demonstrating the competence being assessed. In NVQs, assessors' knowledge and understanding of different cultural and working contexts outside their own experience might be limited, making it difficult for them to ask the right questions and to give sufficient weight to the responses.

For different groups of learners, and particularly for bilingual and disadvantaged learners, the amount and quality of preparation they do, or practice they are given, for interpreting instructions and questions can significantly affect how well they perform. Learners may have different expectations from the assessment than the teacher: where teachers see themselves as offering supportive processes to elicit evidence, for example, learners may see merely a different dimension to a hierarchical power relationship. Perceptions about assessment can therefore affect some learners' responses, especially if their cultural experiences are at odds with unfamiliar assessment processes. Culture, class and gender can affect responses to direct questions, and assessors often treat hesitant, reserved responses differently from assertive, articulate ones, according to their expectations about cultural, gender or class behaviour.

These are complex and controversial areas of assessment practice, but these brief examples show that teachers and programme managers can incorporate an awareness and consideration of the potential for different kinds of bias into planning and implementing the assessment requirements. Preparing learners for assessment, designing different assessment activities, providing feedback and reviewing progress are important areas for discussion and staff development.

Tensions and dilemmas

The complexity of assessment and the changing role of teachers in it, pose dilemmas for all those bodies currently designing and implementing the vocational curriculum. There is a danger that simply passing on the expertise of the awarding bodies, and bodies like the NCVQ, FEFC and FEDA, will not foster a culture where professional insight, knowledge and competence is developed. Guidance and advice increasingly has to make sense to a much wider range of professionals than in the past. It is a feature of all the guidance which is currently emanating from various bodies that these educational, political and technical complexities are not acknowledged. Instead, many assessment processes are taken for granted or treated as if they are straightforward. Emphasis is placed on implementing systems for improving efficiency in assessment.

Although current advice is overwhelmingly technical, it is difficult to ignore some of the wider questions about assessment. These issues lie behind why good and efficient assessment is so difficult to implement well, and teachers can benefit by being aware of them.

Summary

Professional expertise in assessment relies on skills, knowledge and insight into different activities in assessment and their wider implications. Teachers acquire these skills and insights, often without realizing they are doing so, through interaction with colleagues and learners, as well as through interpreting guidance and advice from awarding bodies, books and staff development courses. Learning a new assessment system can be disorienting and can lead teachers to feel disempowered at first. Organizations can use an assessment strategy to ensure that there are developmental processes which enable teachers to share assessment judgements, generate and use exemplars. As well as raising the quality of assessment and making it more efficient, these processes are important staff development opportunities and they supplement formal events. Acknowledging the complexity of assessment is also important if teachers are to develop a sense of ownership over processes for implementing it.

Further reading

Fullan, M (1993) *Change Forces: Probing the depths of educational reform*, Falmer Press, London.

Further Education Development Agency (1995) *Access to Fair Assessment*, FEDA, London.

Further Education Development Agency (1995) *Managing Assessment*, FEDA, London.

Gipps, C (1995) *Beyond Testing: towards a theory of educational assessment*, Falmer Press, London.

Ollin, R and Tucker, J (1994) *The NVQ and GNVQ Assessor Handbook*, Kogan Page, London.

Wolf, A (1993) *Problems in a criterion-based system*, FEDA, London.

Wolf, A (1995) *Competence based assessment*, Open University Press, Buckingham.

9   Designing An
       Assessment Strategy

A strategy for managing and organizing assessment is a new idea for many education and training organizations. A number of colleges and schools have found that designing an assessment policy, and adopting a strategy to achieve it, enables them to respond to the increasingly complex demands which assessment places on them. Changes to assessment systems and practices have brought about extensive curriculum and organizational change. Funding for colleges is linked to learners' achievements and this places demands on organizations to provide effective assessment at different stages. This is taking place in a context of larger class sizes, shorter programmes and increased competition between education and training institutions. Teachers and trainers are using a wider range of approaches to assessment across a much broader scope of learning outcomes than in the past. More learners progress between courses at different levels, or choose modules from different subject areas. Many schools, colleges and universities have franchise arrangements with other institutions, and teachers have to work with a range of awarding bodies. There are different procedures for verifying and moderating learners' work and for assessing and recording achievement. A recent report from the Further Education Development Agency points out that:

> 'The major challenge for... curriculum managers who are providing assessment opportunities on a vast spectrum of programmes with different assessment regimes, is to provide a coherent learning experience for all learners to recognize their prior learning experience and maximize access to assessment opportunities. A central issue is the development of a college assessment policy and a verification framework to ensure the quality of provision and access to fair assessment.' (FEDA, 1995)

A strategy is a systematic series of steps for achieving particular policy goals and targets. It might be based around detailed objectives and targets across the whole institution, for specific programme areas, or for particular groups of learners. These targets are closely related to an assessment policy which outlines how an organizational mission statement affects the principles and practices of assessment in an institution. An assessment policy incorporates aspects of a students' charter, as well as embodying other educational principles valued by an institution. It can also enable institutions to outline how they will meet external requirements. As more institutions experience the processes of funding body inspections and liaise with different awarding body verifiers and examiners, they can harmonize different features of different quality assurance in an overall assessment strategy. An assessment strategy provides an overview of aims for assessment and procedures to implement them. It enables an organization to consider which quantitative and qualitative data needs to be collected, and to develop appropriate systems for collecting this. A strategy helps organizations to decide how this information will be used in evaluation and monitoring.

This chapter aims to:

- outline the main benefits of developing an assessment strategy;
- identify three areas around which a strategy might focus: planning, quality assurance, staff and curriculum development;
- highlight different features of a strategy in each of these three areas.

Benefits of an assessment strategy

In addition to mission statements and standards for monitoring and evaluating quality, some colleges and schools have found it helpful to identify specific targets for assessment and accreditation. These might focus on assessment for particular groups, such as adult learners, or particular approaches, such as using records of achievement. Designing an assessment policy helps an organization to clarify its commitment to accessible, flexible assessment services and processes. A policy which is explicitly focused on the central role of assessment in the vocational curriculum then provides the basis for an organizational strategy for assessment at different levels: curriculum and programme managers, course teams and individual teachers. It also enables learners to receive information about assessment and the part it plays in their learning.

The process of developing a policy does not only help to resolve technical problems in how it is organized. A policy and a strategy for implementing it can also help to raise issues about some of the complexities and controversies which surround assessment, and some of the tensions these can produce. If teachers and curriculum managers are actively involved in a strategy that acknowledges these issues, it is easier to find ways of dealing with them and enabling teachers to have some ownership of external systems.

A framework for developing an assessment strategy

This section proposes a framework for developing an assessment strategy which can achieve aims in three broad areas: planning, quality assurance and staff and curriculum development. A framework can encompass institution-wide standards, codes of practice and processes for monitoring the quality of provision and future issues which need attention. An assessment policy and a strategy for achieving it fits into this framework. The following points include some ideas from FEDA's project 'Managing Assessment'.

Assessment framework

The framework can encompass:

- *an institution's assessment policy*, with aims for assessment relating to its aims and mission;
- *codes of practice* for different assessment provided across the institution, such as diagnostic assessment, accreditation of prior learning, records of achievement;
- *a set of procedures* for assessment in individual programmes which links with aims defined in the policy and with awarding body requirements.

An assessment policy

A policy outlines how organizational aims will be achieved through the management and implementation of assessment. It enables specific targets to be set in different areas. A policy describes:

- *particular principles* which the institution believes should underpin assessment practices;
- *targets* for assessment for all programmes;
- *staff and learners' roles* in assessment, and how these link to promoting achievement, and to the students' charter;
- *procedures for internal verification and moderation*, and the principles which should underpin these;
- *data about learners' achievements* which need to be produced for the Further Education Funding Council, for a local audience to promote the organization and for the publication of student achievement (PISA) for the Department for Education and Employment as part of the 1993 Further and Higher Education Act;
- *quality assurance and control procedures*, and how these link to recording systems and programme monitoring and review.

Codes of practice

These define principles and procedures for providing:

- initial diagnostic assessment;
- assessment and accreditation of prior learning;
- core skills;
- records of achievement;
- access to fair assessment.

Developing an assessment strategy

Some organizations have found it helpful to develop a policy and strategy in discernible stages with particular staff identified to work through these. An initial audit examines how assessment is organized across different programmes. This audit identifies relevant issues from different sources, such as the organizational mission, strategy documents, inspectors' reports and development plans. At this stage, it can be useful to identify staff expertise and interest.

Schools, colleges and universities will have staff who have developed expertise in assessment over a number of years, and in different vocational initiatives. This expertise might hitherto have been unrecognized or taken for granted. The process of developing a strategy can reveal encouraging degrees of interest or practical insights into assessment. Some staff will have studied and researched an aspect of assessment as part of professional development and academic programmes. Others may have taken part in projects related to assessment, while others may have a particular interest in developing their expertise.

Once the initial audits have been carried out, areas for further work and targets can be identified. More detailed audits in key areas are useful here, supported by relevant reports, research findings and background literature. Some organizations have set up working groups or project teams to look at different aspects of assessment in more detail, drawing across the institution for staff and bringing in staff from different levels of seniority.

At this point, reports and views about what needs to be done can lead to the drafting of a policy and different stages in a strategy for implementing it. Figure 9.1 provides an overview of different stages for developing an assessment strategy. The next section is followed by sample checklists which can form the basis for audits and setting targets.

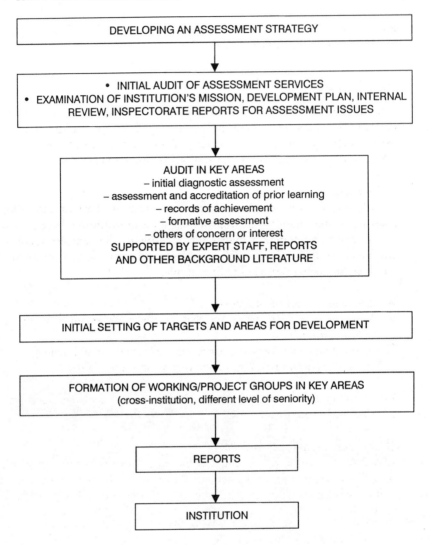

Figure 9.1 *Developing an assessment strategy (based on FEDA 1995)*

Planning assessment

Appointing an assessment coordinator/manager

Some colleges have appointed an assessment and accreditation manager responsible for coordinating assessment and accreditation across the institution. This role can be invaluable in linking different activities in developing an assessment strategy, in motivating staff, and disseminating good practice and developing standardized documentation.

Initial audits

The initial stages of an assessment strategy can enable an organization to examine how assessment is currently offered and the implications of these arrangements for its mission and aims. Audits can begin the process of formulating targets for assessment and identifying staff expertise.

Different assessment activities
In order to rationalize the diverse and confusing array of arrangements for assessing learners in different programmes, some organizations have carried out an audit of different activities for assessment. This enables them to consider the different purposes of assessment and where particular activities are or are not being carried out, for example:

- *planned use of diagnostic assessment;*
- *clarification of targets in an organization's mission,* which require action on assessment, such as:
  - initial guidance for particular groups of learners or all learners;
  - a system of tutorial support and review of learners' progress.

Initial audits identify existing good practice, areas for change, and staff training and development needs.

Documentation and support materials
An audit can examine documentation and other support materials available to staff and learners about assessment, with a view to harmonizing formats and content. It can identify good examples of programme handbooks and other information about assessment.

Some schools and colleges have begun to set up a programme portfolio of exemplars of learners' work. These can be used for staff development as well as for helping learners understand the standard and quality of work they are aiming for. (See Chapter 5 for more detail about using exemplars of learners' work.)

How assessment takes place on vocational programmes
A series of checklists can help identify particular questions to ask in an organizational audit, and for identifying relevant evidence and action which needs to be taken. The checklists which follow in Figure 9.2 are designed to help organizations to find out how assessment is being carried out and what barriers exist to its effectiveness. They are linked to some key areas identified

in this book and developed through the codes of practice for:

- initial diagnostic assessment;
- records of achievement;
- accreditation of prior learning ;
- access to fair assessment;
- core skills.

Disparate policies and processes
A strategy for quality assurance in assessment might begin with an audit of seemingly disparate policies and processes which have implications for how assessment is organized:

- institutional development plan;
- curriculum development plan;
- internal evaluation, monitoring and review procedures;
- inspection reports;
- external examiners' and verifiers' reports.

Setting targets
These enable different areas to be included in a strategy, according to the strengths and weaknesses identified in the audit. Areas might include:

- developing a coherent recording system for collecting different kinds of data;
- using RoAs consistently across the institution;
- developing modular programmes with accreditation of prior learning;
- introducing initial diagnostic assessment in stages across the organization, and drawing on existing good practice.

Resources
Audits can identify existing use of resources for different assessment activities, such as accreditation of prior learning, and examine the implications for staff time, curriculum organization and funding for new developments or for harmonizing existing procedures.

Responsibilities
Developing an assessment strategy relies on the expertise which already exists, but which may not be known to curriculum and senior managers. An audit can identify:

- staff to take on cross-institutional roles, such as coordinators of core skills, records of achievement, internal verification etc;

- staff to be members of working groups, drawn from different curriculum areas and different levels of seniority to consider issues, to identify targets and further work and to monitor the strategy once it is in place;
- internal verifiers and mentors for new staff, or for experienced staff who may be new system of assessment.

Useful reading

Examiners' and verifiers' reports, background literature and research findings, project reports from national bodies, and reports from studies carried out by staff are invaluable sources of information and ideas about managing and implementing different aspects of assessment.

These materials can supplement a central bank of resources and guidance materials from the NCVQ, awarding bodies and the Schools' Curriculum and Assessment Authority (SCAA).

Quality assurance

The demands on organizations for systems to monitor, review and verify the quality of their programmes have probably never been greater. Assessment can provide the focus for quality assurance in all programmes, because it lies at the heart of everything an education or training organization seeks to achieve. An assessment strategy can harmonize a number of activities as part of quality assurance. Setting up systems and methods of monitoring and recording data to respond to external demands is a crucial aspect of quality assurance in assessment. The difficult task for organizational managers is to use the data gathered for external purposes to enhance and develop assessment practice. Processes for quality assurance can therefore play a central role in staff and curriculum development. An assessment strategy can enable an organization to:

- *harmonize disparate procedures* for internal and external verification and evaluation as part of quality assurance across the institution;
- *provide information for teachers and learners* about the role of assessment in learning, and the rules and regulations which govern how it is implemented.

Principles of assessment

An assessment strategy can adopt particular principles which underpin processes for assessment across the organization. Nasta (1994) identifies five principles:

- *Accessibility*: providing learners with clear and transparent information which shows why assessment is carried out, what it will encompass, how and when it will take place.
- *External standards*: showing learners how assessment and achievement relates to the external standards and the verification or examination procedures of the awarding body.
- *Redress*: explaining how learners can seek redress if they feel the assessment process has been poorly or unfairly administered.
- *Consistency*: requiring teachers and curriculum managers to consider how assessment will reflect the intended learning and aims of the programme, and how a course team will approach issues such as grading, timing and type of assignments.
- *Comprehensiveness*: how the assessment process and its accompanying regulations will cover different stages and components of the of the programme, and who will assess which aspects.

An organization may wish to identify others such as breadth of achievement, or educational assessment. Consideration of different principles, especially in light of an organizational mission or ethos, can therefore encompass broader aims for assessment as part of learning as well as operational principles.

Records and systems

Requirements from funding bodies mean that institutions must collect data on learners' achievements at entry to a learning programme, and on exit. The balance between collecting data for external bodies and using it to inform programme monitoring and evaluation is a difficult one. The presentation of achievement in league tables and quantitative data on retention and completion adds further complexity to developing appropriate recording and Management Information Systems. These have to cover the whole institution and individual programme areas. Some institutions have included the following in their recording systems:

- *Outcomes of initial diagnostic assessment*, passed on to appropriate staff, which identify further needs for learning support.
- *Details of the RoAs* learners bring with them.
- *Details of each learner's progress* and achievement in individual units or modules.
- *Costs* of unit certification and APL.
- *Retention* rates.
- *Reasons for withdrawal* when learners leave a programme early.

- *Data which programme teams can access for monitoring and evaluation* purposes such as comparisons between different subject and programme areas, or data about the achievement of cohorts over a period of time as they progress into further and higher education, employment or training.

As well as being important for accountability and evaluation, data collected for different purposes can form the basis for further research by staff on academic in-service programmes, and in curriculum development projects in the organization.

Verification and moderation

Using verification and moderation positively
Verifying and moderating assessment processes and judgements potentially has enormous benefits for the quality of an institution's assessment, particularly in developing professional expertise in assessment. Good systems for verification and moderation can contribute a great deal to staff and curriculum development, as well as ensuring that awarding body requirements are met. An assessment policy can include statements about the principles that underpin processes for internal verification. A strategy then sets out specific objectives, clear roles for different people and a time scale for activities.

Custom and practice
In the past, each awarding body had different arrangements for assuring the standard and quality of learners' achievements and assessors' judgements. Three main features have influenced these arrangements:

- *Validation* – a process of granting approval to a centre to offer a particular qualification.
- *Verification* – ensuring that systems and procedures have been followed correctly and that criteria have been interpreted appropriately.
- *Moderation* – sampling different assessment judgements and evidence in order to compare and standardize them.

There is a considerable overlap in both interpretation and actual practice between verification and moderation. Historically, external examiners, verifiers and moderators represented an awarding body or examination board and acted as arbiters of teachers' assessments. But just as assessment can play an educational, developmental role, so too can the processes of verification and moderation. Although many awarding body verifiers and moderators recognize this, others down play it – hence the variation in practice which exists between awarding bodies such as BTEC, RSA, and CGLI, as well as universities and other examining bodies. In order to support institutions in developing their programmes and to assure their quality, each body has evolved its own version of processes for validation, moderation and verification. These different interpretations of awarding body processes have a strong influence on teachers', managers' and learners' expectations of the particular quality assurance system which affects their qualification.

In NVQs and GNVQs, there has been some harmonization of systems for internal and external verification. These aim to standardize assessment and achievement across awarding bodies, institutions and subject areas. In spite of this, there can still be considerable variation in how different external verifiers and examiners interpret their role: some emphasize a 'checking of systems' approach, others 'moderate' a sample of assessments, while others verify in considerable detail that performance criteria have been met.

An assessment strategy can help managers and teachers:

- *identify the overlap* between these processes;
- *locate validation, verification and moderation in a wider framework* of quality assurance;
- *promote a commitment to rigour* in internal and external verification;
- *promote an ethos of staff development and support* in processes for verifying and moderating assessment processes and decisions.

Internal verification can play a strong formative and developmental role, while external verification needs to satisfy awarding bodies, funding bodies and other external interested parties that systems and standards are consistent and accountable. Both internal and external verification can play a formative and summative role, but the emphasis will be different in each.

Internal verification and moderation

Internal verifiers have two main areas of responsibility – the quality of learners' work and assessors' judgements, and the efficiency and accuracy of assessment systems. They can promote a strong formative ethos for developing professional expertise. They therefore have to:

- *sample the quality and consistency* of assessment practice in a programme;
- *ensure that procedures have been followed* correctly;
- *make judgements about the quality* of colleagues' assessment decisions against national standards;
- *ensure that all records of achievement and portfolios of evidence meet the requirements* of the awarding body;

- *provide advice, guidance and support* to assessors on training and development needs, interpretation of standards, roles and responsibilities in carrying out assessment;
- *clarify formative and summative functions* of verification.

Internal verifiers can work in a particular vocational area across different types of programme at different levels, or across all curriculum areas at one level. However, if internal verification and moderation is to be more than a technical adherence to laid down procedures, any system has to take account of questions about 'dignity and professional self respect, of involvement in decision-making, of skill and training and of the lack of agreed and tested principles and working models as opposed to generalized, well-intentioned official statements' (Radnor and Shaw in Torrance, 1995). It therefore has to incorporate aspects of both verification and moderation. The TVEI Moderation Project, from which the above quote is drawn, showed that 'checking', 'remarking' and 'adjusting marks' is less developmental in raising teachers' standards of assessment than other processes. Radnor and Shaw argue that good moderation is based on:

- *A process of discussion and negotiation*, ultimately accountable to external bodies.
- *Sampling a wide range* of assessment which covers different learning processes and activities.
- *A commitment* to the principle that assessment and moderation skills is a professional obligation.

An external verifier works closely with the internal verifier who is an internal 'guardian' of standards, but is monitoring standards achieved on behalf of the awarding body. In recent years, there appears to have been a shift in NVQs and GNVQs towards a more formal examination of procedures, rather than the more supportive, moderating role which some awarding body verifiers and moderators adopted in the past.

Programme monitoring and evaluation

In many universities, there is a culture of scrutinizing programmes through monitoring and validation procedures. In schools and colleges, the influence of examining and awarding bodies has exerted a different influence on these procedures. An assessment strategy enables an organization to draw on the good practice of different cultures and traditions and to set up systems where assessment is monitored and evaluated as part of quality assurance.

Programme reviews require teams to formally evaluate their programmes, to collate and present information for internal discussion and to identify targets for development. Evidence might include:

- qualitative and quantitative data about learners' achievements;
- external examiners' and verifiers' reports;
- learners' and staff team feedback;
- evaluation of inspectors' and auditors' reports.

When they are carried out supportively and developmentally, reviews can promote understanding between programme teams and promote the sharing of good practice. An assessment strategy can identify how issues raised will be acted on.

Staff and curriculum development

An assessment strategy has led some organizations to consider the demands which the vocational curriculum places on teachers' knowledge and skills in assessment. This has enabled them to consider staff development and training for all staff in the principles and practice of assessment. Examining the demands which assessment places on both new and experienced teachers helps to identify the practical skills, underpinning theory and knowledge about assessment. This also helps in acknowledging some of the complexities inherent in assessment.

The demands which new forms of assessment place on curriculum organization are the focus for an assessment strategy. Core skills, diagnostic assessment, accreditation of prior learning and records of achievement all have implications for programme planning and development. Working out the logistics of setting assignment tasks and deadlines, mapping where different types of assessment are going to take place during the programme, planning tutorial and diagnostic feedback and recording of achievement, are all important areas covered by an assessment strategy. Providing access to fair assessment and minimizing the possibilities of bias is often an overlooked aspect of assessment: a strategy can explicitly address it.

An assessment strategy can enable an organization to:

- *provide a framework for staff development* and professional updating through sharing of practice on different courses and subjects;
- *focus attention on curriculum planning*;
- *enable teachers and managers to be realistic* about what assessment can and cannot achieve;
- *help prevent under- and over-assessment.*

Professional development

Although there are programmes for initial teacher training and continuing professional development for teachers and lecturers in colleges and universities, they are not part of a coherent system for training and updating. There are specific arrangements for initial school teacher training, but continuing professional development for school teachers has been heavily geared to the demands of the National Curriculum. Developing staff to meet the needs of new vocational qualifications can therefore be an ad hoc and piecemeal affair.

As part of their continuing professional development, many teachers undertake further study – often paying for it themselves! Assessment is a popular focus for this study, but although many colleges and schools do take an active and positive interest in this and use the outcomes of the research, others are unaware of the extent of academic study which their staff are doing. An assessment strategy can identify where assessment has been the focus of study or research, either in-house or through other forms of staff education and development, eg BAs, MAs. However, outside formal programmes, many staff have been involved in initiatives in the past such as TVEI, CPVE, and in development projects in their own study and research.

Examples of staff research and in-house projects include:

- A college evaluation of initial diagnostic assessment in literacy and numeracy.
- A school evaluation of GNVQ core skills assessment.
- A college correlation between the 'value added' of modular versus linear GCE A-level science programmes.
- Development of a university document defining criteria for levels in grading.
- A university evaluation of potential bias in business studies assessment.

The widespread use of the NVQ units of competence in assessment (Units D32, D33, D34 and D35 from the Training and Development Lead Body) have had very different responses, with some organizations using them as part of a more developmental process, and others using them more instrumentally for teachers to understand the particular requirements of NVQs. New units of competence are being introduced for teachers assessing GNVQs. From experience of implementing the NVQ units, it seems that they work best if they are part of a more holistic approach to staff development and when they enable teachers to see assessment as a part of a wider process of learning. (See Ollin and Tucker (1994) for a guide on how to make the best use of these awards, and Chapter 8 in this book for discussion about developing professional expertise in assessment).

Programme planning

An assessment strategy which identifies targets for different aspects of assessment and for programme areas can then be addressed by smaller teams.

Assessment plans for a programme show the purposes, timing and scope of assessment and identify where verification and moderation fit into this. Learners and teachers can see where there will be opportunities to review progress and gather evidence. A programme guide can include assessment criteria and guidance and regulations which apply to the programme.

The processes of mapping and auditing the complex requirements and recording systems which teams will need to implement is an important part of strategic planning by programme teams. This requires them to:

- consider how targets in an assessment policy relate to issues and concerns in their area;
- relate the implications of particular targets set by the organization, such as entitlement in a student charter for certain standards of feedback or timing of assessments, to their area;
- consider what information needs to be collected and for which purposes;
- plan for initial diagnostic assessment, accreditation of prior learning, use of records and portfolios of achievement;
- plan the best ways of offering learners opportunities to develop core skills and record achievement in them;
- identify existing and potential barriers to fair assessment for different groups of learners;
- identify staff expertise and areas for development.

Figure 9.2 summarizes activities in an assessment strategy.

The checklists which follow in Figure 9.3 provide a basis for this auditing and planning process.

Managing an assessment strategy

Much has been written about organizational change and the need for staff to feel that they have some ownership of the changes and, be engaged in solving problems, yet much of the guidance and advice for assessing the vocational curriculum is fairly didactic – including this book! Colleges, schools and universities are increasingly required to plan ahead, identify targets and to be strategic, – often in very tight time scales, but strategic planning which relies too heavily on advance planning can be counterproductive. Fullan (1993) argues that in a climate of such complex and almost permanent change, organizations will have 'to reverse traditionally held assumptions about vision and planning'.

He outlines instead three stages which lead to strategic planning, and describes them as a linear sequence: 'Ready, fire, aim'.

Figure 9.2 Activities in an assessment strategy

FOCUS	ACTIVITIES	AREAS	PRINCIPLES	SUCCESSFUL APPROACHES
– relate mission and ethos to learners' achievements – clarify specific targets for assessment and accreditation – identify systems for dealing with assessment	Audit of different services: – diagnostic assessment – targets for improving assessment Audit of assessment in vocational programmes: – initial guidance – selection – in-programme – certification	RoAs Initial diagnostic assessment Recording systems Modular programmes	Comprehensive strategy across staff and provision Staff 'ownership' and professional development	Appointing an assessment manager/coordinator Cross-institution team to develop a policy and strategy Identifying working groups to develop strategy in more detail Identifying relevant reports and literature on assessment
Quality assurance – link procedures for internal and external verification and moderation – provide information for learners and teachers about assessment	Audit of policies and processes – existing good practice – areas of change – documentation – records and systems Positive use of internal verification and moderation	Verification and moderation Monitoring and evaluation Presentation of data documentation	Accessibility of information for learners Clarification of external standards Procedures for redress Developmental processes	Learners' assessment plan Coherent processes for internal verification and moderation Strategic approach to recording systems
Staff and curriculum development – provide framework for staff development in assessment	Audit of research and staff development undertaken by staff in assessment Using D32, 33, 34 etc. positively as part of a coherent programme Identifying targets for training teachers in different areas Linking staff development to processes for internal verification and moderation.	NVQ assessor units Units for planning and assessing GNVQs Academic study or research Internal verification and moderation	Consistency in promoting assessment to reflect educational aims, and a consistent approach to grading, scheduling assessments etc.	Individual team assessment plans and audit of existing arrangements Commitment to teaching learners about assessment Linking in-house staff development to academic and vocational accreditation

Figure 9.3 Areas for an assessment strategy

ACCESS TO FAIR ASSESSMENT	WHOLE ORGANIZATION – person responsible	CURRICULUM AREA – person responsible	PROGRAMME TEAM – person responsible
PLANNING • What issues in equal opportunities does assessment raise across the institution? • What linguistic and cultural barriers are raised in different programme areas?			
STAFF AND CURRICULUM DEVELOPMENT • What staff expertise is there in equal opportunities, linguistic and cultural factors? • What staff development opportunities exist? • How are learners introduced to the purposes and processes of assessment? • What language support is available for bilingual learners? • What cultural and linguistic barriers might be presented by assignments, documentation and inter-personal assessments?			
QUALITY ASSURANCE • What recording systems are there for monitoring the achievement of particular groups? • How are cultural and linguistic factors monitored and evaluated?			
OUTCOMES • Develop targets? • Write a policy? • Design as strategy? • Form a working group? • How do we evaluate the success?			

INITIAL DIAGNOSTIC ASSESSMENT – pre-programme – in-programme	WHOLE ORGANIZATION – person responsible	CURRICULUM AREA – person responsible	PROGRAMME TEAM – person responsible
PLANNING ● What generic processes exist across institution for pre-programme guidance? ● What opportunities are there for subject specific IDA? ● How are time and resources allocated for IDA? ● What particularly useful reports on other reading exist? ● What targets need to be identified?			
STAFF AND CURRICULUM DEVELOPMENT ● What staff development opportunities exist for IDA? ● What staff expertise is there in IDA? ● What potential projects could we develop in IDA?			
QUALITY ASSURANCE ● What information is given to learners about access and entitlement to IDA? ● Is a 'standard' for IDA incorporated in our charter? ● How is information recorded, and passed on, as a result of IDA?			
OUTCOMES ● Develop targets? ● Write a policy? ● Design as strategy? ● Form a working group? ● How do we evaluate the success?			

Figure 9.3 (continued)

CORE SKILLS	WHOLE ORGANIZATION – person responsible	CURRICULUM AREA – person responsible	PROGRAMME TEAM – person responsible
PLANNING ● How are core skills being implemented across the institution? ● What models of implementation and assessment are effective? ● What examples are there of good practice? ● What aspects cause difficulties? ● What particularly useful reports/background literature exists?			
STAFF AND CURRICULUM DEVELOPMENT ● What staff expertise is there in assessing and teaching core skills (eg from BTEC, TVEI, CPVE)? ● Have any staff carried out research or project work in this area? ● What staff development opportunities exist for core skills?			
QUALITY ASSURANCE ● What information is given to learners about core skills? ● How can we improve recording and tracking systems for core skills?			
OUTCOMES ● Develop targets? ● Write a policy? ● Design as strategy? ● Form a working group? ● How do we evaluate the success?			

RECORDS OF ACHIEVEMENT AND PORTFOLIOS	WHOLE ORGANIZATION – person responsible	CURRICULUM AREA – person responsible	PROGRAMME TEAM – person responsible

PLANNING
● How are school leavers' RoAs used across the institution?
● What examples are there of good practice?
● How are RoAs used in:
  a) pre-programme guidance and diagnostic assessment;
  b) during a programme;
  c) on exit?
● What particularly useful reports/background literature exists?			

STAFF AND CURRICULUM DEVELOPMENT ● What staff expertise is there in developing and using RoAs (eg from TVEI, CPVE)? ● What staff development opportunities exist for RoAs (eg. TDLB, professional development programmes eg Certificate in Education, degree or Masters programmes) ● What potential projects could we develop?			
QUALITY ASSURANCE ● What systems are there for recording entry achievements and comparing them to exit ones? ● How are RoAs updated for unit accreditation and on exit? ● How do we evaluate the success of RoAs?			
OUTCOMES ● Develop targets? ● Write a policy? ● Design as strategy? ● Form a working group? ● How do we evaluate the success?			

Figure 9.3 (continued)

ASSESSMENT AND ACCREDITATION OF PRIOR LEARNING	WHOLE ORGANIZATION – person responsible	CURRICULUM AREA – person responsible	PROGRAMME TEAM – person responsible
PLANNING ● What procedures exist in the institution for: a) accreditation of prior *certificated* learning; b) accreditation of prior *experiential* learning? ● How are time and resources allocated to these processes? ● What targets need to be identified? ● What particularly useful reports/background literature exists?			
STAFF AND CURRICULUM DEVELOPMENT ● What staff expertise is there in APL? ● What staff development opportunities exist for APL? ● Have any staff carried out research or project work in this area? ● What potential projects could we develop?			
QUALITY ASSURANCE ● Which of the information and provision outlined in figure 4.3 is available? ● Which information and services still need to be provided? ● What information is given to learners about APL? ● How do we evaluate the success of APL?			
OUTCOMES ● Develop targets? ● Write a policy? ● Design as strategy? ● Form a working group? ● How do we evaluate the success?			

'ready signifies a notion of direction but it is killing to bog down the process with vision, mission and strategic planning, before you know enough about dynamic reality. Fire is action and inquiry, where skills, clarity and learning are fostered. Aim is crystallizing new beliefs, formulating mission and vision statements and focusing strategic planning... Vision and strategic planning come late: if anything they come at step 3, not step 1'

From this viewpoint, an assessment strategy could spark off a process of development rather than being a pre-determined set of targets. By recognizing the complexity of assessment in the vocational curriculum, and the range of skills and insights which teachers need to implement it, a strategy can be formative and developmental as well as meeting external requirements. The balance between development and the need to meet external requirements can, like the balance between formative and summative assessment, be a difficult one. When institution managers and course teams make practical use of the data they collect, it is more likely to become part of useful monitoring and evaluation procedures. If data is not used, or only collated for external requirements, it is unlikely to help teams identify strengths and weaknesses and plan future changes and developments.

Acknowledging the complexity of assessment

The complexity of new assessment regimes can lead an assessment strategy to focus on the technicalities of organizing and implementing assessment to meet external requirements. Other chapters have tried to show that many of the difficulties which teachers and institutions might face in organizing assessment coherently across different programmes, arise from fundamental tensions in both its historical development and its implementation. An assessment strategy for staff and curriculum development needs to acknowledge this, and take account of different technical and educational issues which might affect:

- *the design* of assessment systems;
- *teachers' interpretations of what is required* of them;
- *the need to train and socialize new teachers* into different assessment regimes and systems, both by experiencing the processes of NVQs and GNVQs themselves through the units of competence, for example, and by taking part in moderation and discussion with colleagues about criteria, standards and assessment decisions;
- *inherent tensions*, particularly between the formative use of assessment to support and enhance learning, and the summative function of certifying and selecting students for progression;
- *lack of familiarity* with new requirements and changes to procedures and systems implemented at speed.

159

See Chapter 10 for further discussion of tensions and dilemmas in assessment.

Summary

The technical and educational complexities of assessment mean that increasing numbers of education and training organizations are adopting a strategic approach to the management and implementation of assessment. Using processes and recording systems for quality assurance, such as verification and moderation, or collection of different data, as positively and developmentally as possible can help organizations consider educational aims for assessment as well as meeting external requirements. This explicitly elevates the promotion of learning and achievement above the level of rhetoric.

Further reading

Ecclestone, K (1994) *Understanding Assessment*, NIACE, Leicester.

Fullan, M (1993) *Change Forces: probing the depths of educational reform*, Falmer Press, London.

Further Education Development Agency (1994) *Implementing GNVQs – a manual*, FEDA, London.

Further Education Development Agency (1995) *Assessment Issues in Further Education*, FEDA, London

Further Education Development Agency (1995) *Access to fair assessment*, FEDA, London

Further Education Development Agency (1995) *Developments in value-added*, FEDA, London.

Nasta, T (1994) *How to Design a Vocational Curriculum*, Kogan Page, London.

Ollin, R and Tucker, J (1994) *The NVQ and GNVQ Assessor Hardbook*, Kogan Page, London.

Torrance, H (ed) (1995) *Evaluating Authentic Assessment*, Open University Press, Buckingham.

10   Tensions and Dilemmas
in Assessment

A recurring theme throughout this book has been the social, educational and political power of assessment which produces a number of attendant dilemmas and complexities. There are high political stakes in the design and use of assessment throughout the education system: it is used to certify and select people, to ration places at higher levels of education and training, as a factor in decisions about levels of funding for individual organizations, and to make institutions accountable. It is often these purposes which dominate teachers' and learners' perceptions about assessment. They also shape the way that the vocational curriculum and its various assessment regimes are organized and implemented. This has implications for how managers and teachers approach the whole issue of assessment. If political and funding requirements are emphasized at the expense of broader, more educational aims for assessment, summative, external purposes of assessment will dominate whatever the rhetoric says otherwise.

Assessment potentially has many positive effects on learning and on learners' motivation. At its most benign, it can help learners describe their past achievements, recognize new ones and make informed choices about what they should do next. It can have powerful and transforming effects on learners' ability to diagnose their own strengths and weaknesses, and to assess their own progress and independence in learning. Once learners can do this, they have the skills and motivation to seek assessment in other settings, whether in a learning programme or at work. Asking for feedback and judging one's own progress become second nature. All these positive features are given a high profile in the publicity which surrounds recent initiatives in the vocational curriculum. At its most negative, though, assessment can undermine motivation for learning or lead to failure and drop-out. It can make teachers and learners preoccupied with 'meeting the requirements'. This creates new manifestations of 'teaching to the test'. At its most tedious, it can be irrelevant to learning and become a mechanistic and time consuming process of amassing vast amounts of evidence.

Unless assessment is coherently planned and organized explicitly with a view to achieving positive educational purposes as well as conforming to external requirements, existing forms of assessment may actually be incompatible with these aims. This danger is compounded by relying too much on providing teachers and assessors with very extensive, detailed guidance about how to interpret and use assessment criteria, and how to implement the administrative procedures surrounding assessment. Well-presented external guidance is crucial in helping teachers, assessors and learners interpret the requirements, but it cannot, on its own, enable them to arrive at their own understanding about how assessment can play a positive role in learning. For this to happen, curriculum designers, awarding bodies and managers of institutions have to develop processes which allow teachers to share judgements, locate assessment in learning activities and to collaborate with learners to interpret tasks and standards.

Good, effective assessment is hard to do. Even experienced teachers find changes to a system, or to their own role in it, difficult. There are complex technical processes to implement as well as complex, and sometimes controversial, principles underpinning them. It is also clear, though, that the goal of raising learners' achievements and abilities to learn are powerful reasons for pursuing better assessment.

This chapter outlines some of the main difficulties and dilemmas which affect organizations' and teachers' attempts to plan and manage assessment strategically. It considers three main issues:

- different theories about assessment and learning which affect how assessment is 'designed and implemented;
- the scope and range of assessment which are seen as important;
- the effects of attempts to ensure valid and reliable assessment.

Assessment: science or social construction?

Conflicting theories about how people learn and how their learning should be measured lie at the heart of many tensions in how assessment is used. Until recently, there have been few links made between different approaches to assessment and the types of learning we want learners to achieve. Current research into GNVQ core skills by the NCVQ and into formative assessment in the National Curriculum, is now making explicit and interesting links between the effects of assessment on learning, and, in turn, how teachers might enhance the quality and effectiveness of learning. Two underlying theories influence how assessment is implemented in GNVQs and NVQs.

Defining and measuring behaviours and outcomes

One theory comes from a 'positivist' tradition in science and research. It suggests that knowledge and behaviours can be described, observed and measured in logical and rational ways. Technical procedures can be designed and refined over time to make the process of defining learning outcomes more efficient and more able to reflect the reality of human behaviour. In turn, improved definitions of learning outcomes can then be assessed through similarly logical and efficient means. In assessment, this view has been heavily influenced by a history of psychometric testing with its roots in notions that certain abilities and traits are 'fixed' and can therefore be reliably measured. In this positivist tradition, behaviourist psychology has promoted models of learning based on the outcomes of observable behaviour.

In recent years, a positivist viewpoint has moved away from the influence of psychometric testing of certain traits and abilities to encompass a wider range of human behaviour. Positivist approaches are also used to define attributes like independence and autonomy, skills of problem solving and group work. These behaviours are seen as being transferable to other contexts and situations – hence the emphasis on core skills and transferable skills in many qualifications. These beliefs underpin the processes that are used to derive standards of competence and functional analysis in NVQs, and similar procedures to map the scope, learning outcomes and assessment criteria in GNVQs.

Constructing learning

The other theory comes from a quite different social and psychological tradition. It is based on a view that knowledge and behaviour are socially constructed and not, therefore, automatically observable, transferable and measurable. Instead, assessment is affected by the ways that learners interact with the assessment tasks, the contexts where these processes take place, and the influence of the assessor. Assessments and their outcomes are therefore constructed in social interactions and have different meanings for those involved in them. From this standpoint, it cannot be assumed that learners automatically transfer their behaviour to other tasks and contexts. Rather, much more attention has to be paid to helping learners construct their own interpretations of assessment and to be effective learners.

It also means that instead of being a process of interpreting and 'passing on' fixed specifications, assessment is a process of constructing and reconstructing ideas about the knowledge and skills being assessed. In turn, assessment designers have their own constructions about assessment which are embodied in the specifications. Teachers and learners therefore have to engage in dialogue and collaboration to make sense of the 'constructions' embodied in the specifications, so that they arrive at their own understanding of what is required. This is necessary if the assessment is going to have a positive effect on learning. A constructivist viewpoint believes that a learner's ability to perform well is dependent on context, their motivation and their perceptions of how relevant the task is. Their performance is affected by interaction, support, good formative feedback. Assessment has to give people the chance to show what they can do, to maximize their learning for their best performance. This is clearly much more complex than helping learners meet the requirements – 'teaching to the test'. Instead of being neutral or impartial, a constructivist viewpoint believes that the outcomes and processes of assessment are affected by:

- the *context*;
- *learners' perceptions* of relevance of the assessment task;
- *relationships* between assessor and learner;
- perceptions about the *purpose of assessment*.

Behaviourist psychology Positive science	Cognitive psychology	Humanist psychology Constructivism
Influences	**Influences**	**Influences**
Socialization through rewards and punishments	Rational understanding	Self-motivation
	Specifying improvement and achievement	Constructing achievement
Effects	**Effects**	**Effects**
Systems	Training learners to assess	Agreeing strategies jointly
Explicit definitions of traits and behaviours	Communicating errors	Mutual review of progress
External standards and targets		Close learner/ assessor relationship

Figure 10.1 *Theories about learning and their influence on assessment*

The positivist and constructivist theories are not necessarily in conflict with each other, but they tend to emphasize different things. A positivist approach to assessment stresses the importance of effective systems for defining what is to be assessed, observable outcomes and transferability. A constructivist approach emphasizes the importance of interaction, and the effects of social and personal factors on the success, or otherwise, of assessment.

Formative versus summative assessment

The tension between using assessment to enhance learning and the need to create efficient and credible summative assessment reveals the influence of the two different views of learning, although the distinction is not clear cut. Constructivism and the desire to help learners be active and effective learners reveals itself, for example, in developments in records of achievement, self-assessment and diagnostic assessment. Theories about effective learning in GNVQ core skills and in the grading criteria reveal constructivist ideas about the importance of negotiation and the need to foster learners' deep involvement in the processes of learning.

At the same time, the heavy emphasis in both NVQs and GNVQs on systems for defining outcomes and criteria, shows the powerful influence of positivism and behaviourist ideas about how learning and assessment should be measured. At times, the specifications for assessment might be too burdensome for the types of collaboration which are at the heart of constructivist ideas about learning.

Defining the scope of assessment

The vocational curriculum illustrates tensions in relation to the scope of assessment. On the one hand, there is a desire to define a wide range of achievements in order to motivate learners and to make assessment more relevant to them. On the other is a need to make assessment reflect outcomes which are valid and useful for stakeholders, such as employers and other education and training organizations. Decisions about what is to be assessed and how the outcomes, will be recorded pose both technical and philosophical dilemmas. These affect which skills, attributes and knowledge are seen as important, and which methods will be used to assess and record them. As a result, controversy arises over processes for defining learning outcomes, and the various bodies who should – and should not – be involved in assessment.

Technical issues

Some skills and attributes may not be amenable to standardized testing since they are hard to define. Assessing them may rely on teachers and assessors having extensive knowledge of learners. These difficulties pose technical questions for the designers of assessment. When teachers are extensively involved in tutorial reviews and in helping learners provide evidence of achievements from life and work experiences, for example, there are difficulties in ensuring reliable assessments about the quality, scope and presentation of evidence.

There are also technical issues in assuring validity. Assessment of a wide range of personal skills and qualities has to be fair to learners. It also has to enable an external audience to infer the transferability of these outcomes of learning to other contexts. From a constructivist point of view, there are questions about how teachers' assessments of learners' personal skills and qualities are affected by the particular context and the teacher's knowledge of the learner in other settings. Many core skills – such as problem solving, working with others, being an independent learner – are not easily transferable since they are heavily dependent on the context where they are shown. Someone excellent at team work with a particular group working on a task they enjoy, for example, is not automatically excellent in an alien context with a difficult or unenjoyable task. To counteract some of these difficulties, a positivist approach aims to make the specifications of context and 'typical' evidence as clear and detailed as possible.

Deciding what to assess

Assessment systems may include certain personal skills and qualities and exclude others. For some commentators, these decisions represent philosophical or political dilemmas rather than technical ones. Those who support a beneficial role for assessment argue that 'achievement' should encompass a wide range of learning outcomes, because this enables learners to demonstrate attributes for employment and further and higher education. Assessment of these attributes is also made public rather than being the subject of references or informal comments. Defining a wide range of skills and attributes elevates the processes of learning to a central place in the vocational curriculum and enables formative and diagnostic assessment to take on an important role in learning.

However, increasing the scope of summative assessment also poses dilemmas about which attributes are assessed – cooperation, initiative and team work are often included, for example, while awareness of social justice, critical analysis or political activity might be left out. In NVQs, particular values and ethics may be built into the standards because they are seen as important in occupational competence, even though they may also be contentious or hard to assess.

Widening definitions of achievement can have other effects. Some of the activities and interests which learners might define as achievements might fulfil the motivating aspects of records of achievement and portfolios, but they might also be frowned upon by employers or other audiences. For adults compiling a portfolio of life and work experience, there can be disappointment when their achievements do not match pre-defined outcomes.

Other commentators raise questions about the implications of formally assessing a very extensive range of attributes. Assessment may take on an over-dominant role in a vocational curriculum, where almost every aspect of behaviour and life experience is potentially under the scrutiny of assessors and awarding bodies. Other questions concern the purpose of defining more outcomes for learning and assessment. In commenting on developments in records of achievement, Hargreaves argues that: 'in records of achievement, we have a system designed to enhance [learners'] motivation but without any broadly based political or professional discussion or agreement about what pupils are being motivated towards' (Hargreaves, in Murphy and Torrance, 1987).

Definitions of learning outcomes and decisions about whether they are formatively or summatively assessed are therefore subject to controversial political influences as well as posing technical dilemmas.

Creating valid and reliable assessment

'The accurate and valid assessment of standards... represents a complex set of professional challenges. The seeming precision and accuracy of published quantitative data mask the difficulty of adequately selecting or determining and representing the range of criteria which truly reflects educational standards' (Cohen cited by Murphy and Torrance, 1988).

'Perfect transparency is not to be had, however detailed one's definition, and searching for it merely produces atomized objectives in a forest of verbiage' (Wolf, 1993).

The history of assessment shows that designers of assessment have constantly grappled with the difficulty of reconciling reliability and validity. Although the emphasis given to each might vary in different types of qualification, complete validity and reliability are extremely difficult – if not impossible – to attain. When assessment has high political stakes, such as in GCE A-level and GCSE results or the standards of degrees, comparability between assessors, awarding bodies and institutions becomes the focus of debate. When the ability to create self-monitoring and motivated learners is the issue, the fairness of assessment and its correlation to the particular skill or attribute being assessed is more important. Issues of standardization between assessors and the need to validly assess a wide scope of learning outcomes are therefore a source of technical difficulty. If assessment is made more reliable, its scope narrows to assess easily measurable outcomes. Taken to extremes, the most reliable assessment does not measure important aspects of learning. If it is made more valid, the specifications grow to encompass the desired range of outcomes and the evidence which are needed to infer validity. As a result, valid assessment becomes burdensome and mechanistic.

In spite of these dilemmas, strategies for promoting reliability, such as cross-moderation and joint marking, can bring more standardization to assessment designed for maximum validity, and more precise and careful specifications can add validity to assessment designed for maximum reliability. But the tension between the two cannot be resolved by technical refinements alone. Constructivist approaches to learning and assessment can supplement technical improvements to assessment. Diagnostic assessment and the collaboration between learners and teachers outlined in Chapter 5 support the educational aims which assessment can achieve. Without this balance, there is a danger that new forms of assessment become too cumbersome and mechanistic, and ultimately, undermines the motivation and deep learning they are intended to promote.

Summary

The history of the vocational curriculum illustrates emerging themes in assessment over the past 15 years, as outlined in Chapter 3. Many of them represent a better understanding about how to use assessment positively. As this chapter shows, they also illustrate some long-running tensions. This chapter concludes by highlighting the main tensions which currently manifest themselves in the education and training system, and particularly in the vocational curriculum. They are not automatically in conflict with each other but they can pose dilemmas for the designers of assessment and the managers and teachers who have to implement it.

Tensions

External accountability/public credibility v. assessment to enhance learning for both teachers and learners
The need for organizations to conform to external specifications as a means of standardizing assessment and assuring accountability, and the need to enable teachers and learners to maximize formative and diagnostic assessment.

A wide range of outcomes v. motivation for learning
The need to assess a much wider range of outcomes so that employers and education and training institutions can infer competence, employability and learning potential with a need to make assessment meaningful to learners so that they are motivated to raise their achievements.

Standardized assessment v. individual interpretations and constructions
The need to standardize assessment systems and processes across different subject traditions, sectors and institutions, with the need for teachers to share their interpretations with learners and colleagues.

168

Efficient use of resources v. time to use assessment positively
The need to implement specifications and processes for assessment efficiently in a climate of declining resources, with a need for teachers to work with learners and colleagues to make assessment effective and fair.

Many of the technical procedures to assure the quality of assessment and to implement fair, valid and reliable assessment can have positive effects when they are managed well. An assessment strategy can concentrate on implementing the requirements specified by external bodies and find the most efficient ways of doing this, but if organizations are to offer educationally meaningful assessment, a strategy will also need to acknowledge the complexity of assessment and the necessary professional skills to implement it. In light of the tensions outlined in this chapter, a strategy can:

- *clarify* an organization's own purposes and aims for assessment;
- *harmonize* different processes for different types of assessment as much as possible across the organization;
- *recognize* the resource implications of educational and developmental approaches to assessment;
- *balance* external rigour and accountability with a commitment to formative and diagnostic assessment;
- *share* good practice, *develop* exemplars and *moderate* assessment in ways which enhance professional skills, confidence and commitment.

These aims cannot, of course, counter the tensions on their own. This book has aimed to provide practical insights into how assessment might be managed and implemented, taking into account some of the reasons why this can be difficult. In doing this, it proposes that awarding bodies, teachers, managers of education and training organizations, learners themselves and those involved in research and professional development continue to address the technical theoretical and political complexities of assessment. The goal of motivating and meaningful assessment is the key to creating a vocational curriculum which really is part of life-long learning.

Further reading

Murphy, R and Torrance, H (1988) *The Changing Face of Educational Assessment*, Open University Press, Buckingham.
Wolf, A (1995) *Competence Based Assessment*, Open University Press, Buckingham.
Wolf, A (1993) *Problems with a Criterion Based System*, FEDA, London.

Glossary and Index of Terms

The glossary provides a list and brief definitions of the important terms and acronyms used in the text. Page references are given for the main discussion of these terms.

Accreditation the formal process leading to the recognition of successful achievement through the granting of an award, or part of an award. Unit accreditation, for example, is offered in some qualifications where learners have successfully achieved the learning outcomes of a unit or module.

ALIS A-level information system used to collect data about entry qualifications and final achievement in A-level grades. (p.77)

APEL accreditation of prior experiential learning. This enables learners to seek formal recognition (accreditation) of relevant learning from past work and life experience. (p.60)

APL accreditation of prior learning, a generic term that encompasses both the accreditation of prior experiential learning and the accreditation of prior certificated learning. (pp.56–61)

Assessment the judgement of evidence of learning and achievement, submitted by learners for a particular purpose. (pp.9–20)

Attainment targets the broad objectives outlined in the school National Curriculum that set out the knowledge, skills and understanding pupils must acquire. (p.50)

BTEC Business and Technology Education Council. It has merged recently with the University of London Examination Board. (p.30)

CAT credit accumulation and transfer, the process by which qualifications and past achievements are awarded educational 'credits' so that learners can transfer between courses and programmes. (p.47)

Certificate   the formal document issued to learners by an awarding or examining body and which confirms achievements.

CGLI   City and Guilds of London Institute. (p.30)

CPVE   the Certificate of Pre-Vocational Education. (pp.32–33, 92)

Competence   the ability to perform job and task functions in a work setting or in simulations. (pp.111–112)

Core skills   transferable or 'essential' skills for life and work roles such as application of number, problem-solving, group and team work, communication, information technology and evaluation of own work. (pp.107–110)

Course   a curriculum, usually based on a number of compulsory and option elements that are studied in a set sequence over a set period of time. (p.46)

Credit   a measure of the volume and level of learning achieved in a module or discrete element of a course or programme. Credits can be accumulated towards whole qualifications. (pp.52–53)

Credit accumulation   the process of achieving and certificating separate components of a qualification over a period of time. (p.47)

Credit transfer   the recognition of credits gained in one qualification system towards some or all of the requirements in a different qualification system. (p.47)

Criterion   a single statement that describes how to assess learning outcomes to the required standard and quality of performance.

Criteria   a number of statements that describe how to assess learning outcomes to the required standard and quality of performance. (pp.51–52)

Criterion-referenced assessment   a system of assessment that measures learners' achievements against external definitions of the required standard, type and context of performance. (pp.18–19)

DfEE   Department for Education and Employment. (p.26)

Diagnostic assessment   the process of finding out learners' existing strengths and weaknesses in order to offer learning support and guidance about future needs. This can take place before the start of a learning programme and is a crucial part of the teaching and learning process during a programme. (pp.76–81)

Element of competence   the smallest specification of competence in an NVQ statement of competence. Elements are accumulated to make up a unit of competence. (p.35)

FEDA   Further Education Development Agency, a national curriculum development and research body that carries out research projects and management and staff development for further education and sixth form colleges. (p.44)

FEFC   Further Education Funding Council, the national body responsible for funding and external quality assessment for institutions in the further education sector offering FEFC-funded programmes.

Formative assessment   assessment designed to diagnose learning needs, barriers to learning and achievements. This enables teachers to give feedback to learners about the quality of their work and future targets. Formative assessment does not contribute to formal grading or final assessment. (pp.12–13, 93–95)

Functional analysis   the process of analysing the key purpose and related occupational functions in a broad occupational area.

GCE   General Certificate of Education. (p.4)

GCSE   General Certificate of Secondary Education. (p.4)

GNVQ   General National Vocational Qualification, a broad-based vocational qualification assessed to national standards and which confirms achievement of general and core skills, knowledge and understanding that underpins a range of occupations in a related area. (pp.35–37)

Guidance   an impartial process that helps learners to consider their best options in light of past experiences and future aspirations. As part of assessment, guidance can be used to help learners assess their prior achievements and to consider the next step. (pp.73–75)

Individual action plan   a set of learning targets and needs negotiated between learners and the organization providing the learning programme. (p.13)

Ipsative assessment   assessment that measures a learner's achievements against criteria determined by her or his previous performance (self-referenced assessment). (pp.19–20)

LCCIEB   London Chamber of Commerce and Industry, an awarding body. (p.30)

Learning outcomes   statements of expected achievements that cover practical skills and competencies, knowledge, cognitive and intellectual skills, personal skills, attributes and qualities at different levels of complexity and across different contexts and situations. These outcomes can be specified in detail or in general statements and are usually accompanied by criteria for assessing them. (pp.50–51)

LEC   Local Enterprise Council. Scottish equivalent of TEC (see below).

Moderation   the process of comparing and confirming assessment decisions and judgements between assessors in order to standardize assessment decisions. This can be carried out between teachers and by awarding and examining bodies and there is an overlap between moderation and verification. (pp.126, 147–149)

Module   a unit of learning and assessment that is usually free-standing and can therefore be taken separately or in conjunction with other modules. (pp.49–50)

Moderator   an external assessor appointed by an awarding or examining body to monitor standards achieved on a set of vocational courses or programmes. (p.147)

NCVQ   National Council for Vocational Qualifications. (p.30)

NOCN   National Open College Network, an accrediting and awarding body for adult education programmes and many of the Access to higher education courses. (p.31)

National Record of Achievement   a national system for recording achievement from school through life and encompassing different qualifications. (p.88)

NVQs   National Vocational Qualifications are accredited by the NCVQ and offered by a range of awarding bodies and covering a wide range of occupational areas and jobs. (pp.34–35)

NTETs National Targets for Education and Training, a set of agreed objectives set by government for increasing participation in the vocational education and training system and for raising achievement levels in academic and vocational qualifications. (p.3)

Norm-referenced assessment a system of assessment that measures learners' performance and ascribes a standard to it by comparing it to the performance of other candidates in the same cohort. (pp.17–18)

Occupational standards descriptions of types and levels of competence in a job role which are established by a Lead Body in an occupational area in order to create NVQs. (p.34)

Performance criteria the specific criteria that establish the range, scope and quality of performance that candidates must show in order to gain elements and units of competence in an NVQ. (p.36)

PISA published information on student achievement, required by the DfEE from colleges and schools about achievement in qualifications. (p.2)

Portfolio a collection of evidence of achievement such as assignments, projects and artefacts made by learners in learning programmes or from other life and work experiences and which can be submitted for formal assessment and accreditation. (p.91)

Progression the development and accumulation of skills and achievements through successive learning opportunities and the opportunity to move on to another related stage of learning.

Record of achievement a document that records formal and informal achievements. (p.89)

Reliability assessment that is designed to ensure that the same range of results gained by learners could be reproduced in a different cohort of learners who are deemed to have similar 'abilities'. Assessment designed for reliability aims to enable assessors to standardize their judgements against those of other assessors. (pp.22–23)

RSA Royal Society of Arts. The RSA examination board is now completely independent from the RSA. (p.30)

SCAA   School Curriculum and Assessment Authority. (p.44)

Summative assessment   the formal assessment process that enables
            assessors and verifiers from awarding bodies to judge
            evidence of achievement submitted by learners in order to
            determine a final result or grade in a module or unit, or for
            a whole qualification. (pp.14–15, 95–96)

TEC   Training and Enterprise Council (England and Wales). (p.33)

TVEI   Training and Vocational Education Initiative. (pp.31–32, 92)

Quality assurance   the processes and procedures developed by
            organizations to ensure the quality of learning
            programmes, assessment and accreditation. (pp.54–56,
            99–100, 145)

Unit of competence   a component of an NVQ that is broken down into
            elements of competence. A unit represents a discrete aspect
            of competence and can be accredited separately and
            accumulated over time towards a full NVQ. (p.36)

Validity   assessment that is designed to measure accurately a range of
            learning outcomes. Assessment designed for validity aims
            to enable different interested parties to infer that these
            outcomes have been achieved and that learners could
            reproduce them in other similar situations in future.
            (pp.23–24)

Verification   the process of internal and external monitoring carried out
            by awarding bodies and institutions to ensure that
            assessment and accreditation procedures are being
            correctly and systematically adhered to and that standards
            are being achieved against set criteria. Guidelines for
            verification in NVQs and GNVQs are issued by the
            awarding bodies. (pp.126, 147–149)

Work-based assessment   the measurement of performance in the
            workplace, usually by a work-place assessor. (p.112)